WORD NERDS UNITE!

THE FASCINATING STORIES BEHIND 200 WORDS AND PHRASES

WEBB GARRISON

NELSON
BOOKS

An Imprint of Thomas Nelson

Published in Nashville, Tennessee, by Nelson Books, an imprint of Thomas Nelson. Nelson Books and Thomas Nelson are registered trademarks of HarperCollins Christian Publishing, Inc.

Thomas Nelson titles may be purchased in bulk for educational, business, fundraising, or sales promotional use. For information, please e-mail SpecialMarkets@ThomasNelson.com.

Any internet addresses, phone numbers, or company or product information printed in this book are offered as a resource and are not intended in any way to be or to imply an endorsement by Thomas Nelson, nor does Thomas Nelson vouch for the existence, content, or services of these sites, phone numbers, companies, or products beyond the life of this book.

ISBN 978-1-4003-3799-6 (audiobook)
ISBN 978-1-4003-3798-9 (eBook)

Library of Congress Cataloging-in-Publication Data is on File

ISBN 978-1-4003-3797-2

Printed in the United States of America

23 24 25 26 27 LBC 5 4 3 2 1

CONTENTS

CHAPTER 1

THE WORLD OF ENTERTAINMENT

From the stage to screen, the world of entertainment has contributed to popular speech, while simultaneously drawing from it. Sample words and phrases from this rich vein of speech will often help you "to know what the play is."

Barnstormer
Behind the Scenes
Blockbuster
Cameo Role
Circus
Double Take
Flip Side
Green-Eyed Monster

BARNSTORMER

In the early days of traveling theater, third-rate companies didn't get the best facilities. Many had to settle for almost any empty building. Some held one-night performances in barns. Such a group didn't stay anywhere long. Entertainers stormed from place to place, sometimes waiting for horses and cows to be moved out before a stage could be improvised.

A candidate for office who races from one spot to another, addressing small crowds, has a lot in common with a theatrical barnstormer. From amateurish performers and hack politicians, the term is attached to anyone who moves around a lot without getting much done.

BEHIND THE SCENES

Development of the theater proceeded rapidly during the long reign of England's Queen Elizabeth I. However, more attention was given to scripts and actors than to stage settings. Most performances took place before a backdrop of simple curtains.

Subsequent kings James I and Charles I encouraged free spending in the arts. Under their sponsorship, craftsmen began making elaborate painted slides and hangings for backdrops on a stage. Such pieces, which often represented landscapes, were known simply as *scenes*.

In many plays and operas, important action was not represented on the stage; instead it was simply reported to the audience. This was especially the case with murders and executions, which were often treated as having taken place between acts.

Patrons joked about the fact that many events occurred not on the stage, but "behind the scenes." Hence real-life action hidden from the public came to be described by the term born in the theater.

BLOCKBUSTER

Any time a blockbuster movie or novel is released, lines are sure to form. Producers and publishers know that the glow won't last long, so they want to cash in while they can.

The earliest blockbusters stayed in the news for month after month during World War II. The original *blockbuster* was a high-explosive bomb that could level an entire block.

Eventually, anything that made a considerable impact, like a spectacularly successful enterprise or production, took the name of the most powerful bomb before the advent of nukes.

CAMEO ROLE

Seashells and gemstones often have several layers that include two or more hues. Long ago, artisans learned to take advantage of this factor by carving in such fashion that a raised central figure or figures of a different color rose from the background.

A cameo engraved in this way doesn't have to be rare and costly in order to be beautiful and prized. Many that are hawked on the streets of Rome and other European cities are inexpensively exquisite, though tiny.

Transferred to the world of entertainment, the name of small but lovely jewelry became the term for a bit part played by a notable performer. On the stage, in the movies, and in television, many producers vie for viewers by including cameo roles that feature persons with famous names.

CIRCUS

Life under the Caesars wasn't centered entirely upon war and conquest. Partly to keep common folk contented, rulers built in the capital city a vast sports arena. Shaped like a huge circle, or *circus,* Rome's biggest structure gained international fame as the *Circus Maximus.*

Males and females were separated at most public assemblies. Not so when they went to the *Circus Maximus.* There they mingled freely and saw many lavish spectacles.

Long used to designate any structure built for sport or entertainment, the Roman name shifted from buildings to performances staged in them. When Phineas T. Barnum added acrobats and jugglers to long-traditional equestrian acts, the traveling circus was born. Today's circuses focus on astonishing human talents rather than acts with animals, but these death-defying performers aren't any less hypnotizing.

DOUBLE TAKE

Have you ever been stopped short by a glimpse of something and didn't believe what you saw? That common experience calls for a second and closer look—a double take.

Whether working on a set or in a studio, many a director has called for the camera to take another look at a snippet of action or a full scene. Every take is on trial until it meets the director's approval. When footage is judged unsatisfactory by an on-the-spot decision, a double take is in order.

Erupting from lingo of the entertainment world, *double take* has come to mean anything deserving a second, or better, look.

FLIP SIDE

There is a belief in the working of opposite cosmic forces in terms of yin and yang. Many people, versed in technology, say that every argument and each set of principles has a "flip side."

Though the expression is too firmly entrenched in speech to face an early demise, the technology that produced it is virtually obsolete. Tape cassettes wreaked havoc in the phonograph record industry; compact discs sounded its death knell, followed by MP3 players and, today, streaming music.

But in its heyday, the revolving platter ruled popular music in the Western world. Practically every song that went to the top of the charts was accompanied by another that didn't rival it in popularity. Cut into the reverse face of a record, this musical hitchhiker was noticeably different from its companion. Which meant that practically every record had its flip side—a second recording that gave listeners a quite different impression from that produced by the first.

GREEN-EYED MONSTER

Theatergoers did not realize what a good thing they had when the plays of Shakespeare first hit the stage. But it took only a few encounters with his work for patrons to realize that the playwright talked and wrote like no one before.

Casting about for a vivid way to describe jealousy, the Bard of Avon remembered that many cats have green eyes. Not necessarily correctly, he seems to have considered cats to be cruel and vindictive.

Therefore, in *Othello* (Act III), he called jealousy *the green-eyed monster*—comparing it with a cat that, to a human, appears to play with the bird or mole it has captured and is about to eat.

HANDWRITING ON THE WALL

Ancient Babylon flourished under the rule of King Nebuchadnezzar. But his son and successor, Belshazzar, proved weak and profligate. Ignoring all standards, he once drank heavily from holy vessels seized from the Temple in

Jerusalem. A mysterious hand appeared after this act of sacrilege and, to the astonishment of the king, wrote four strange words on the wall of the banquet room.

Only the Hebrew prophet, Daniel, could interpret the mysterious message. He boldly told the ruler that they spelled disaster for him and for his nation. Soon afterward Belshazzar was defeated and slain, just as Daniel said.

Religious dramas of the Middle Ages often included vivid interpretations of events in the ancient banquet hall. Viewers of such pageants sat enthralled as they watched the writing of the strange warning to a king. As a result, any threat of impending doom is still known as "handwriting on the wall."

HIT

Authors and publishers, along with actors and producers and songwriters, want nothing so much as a hit.

That is precisely what a contestant engaged in a predecessor to baseball hoped to get when given an opportunity to swing a bat.

A good, solid hit on the playing field meant an opportunity to advance and maybe even to score. Consequently, onlookers and athletes applied the term to any enterprise that has a successful, popular following.

LIMELIGHT

Lighting was one of the chief problems of the early theater. In the time of Shakespeare, all available devices were crude and ineffective.

Actors, playwrights, and theatergoers were delighted when Thomas Drummond devised a new source of light in 1816. A cylinder of lime was heated to incandescence by a flame, and when placed behind a lens or in front of a reflector, the limelight proved to be intensely bright.

The brightness made it ideal for use in making a star performer more visible. As long as one remained in it, audience attention was riveted.

Competition for a place in the limelight soon became intense. Consequently, it came to label any conspicuous spot—whether flooded by one of Thomas Drummond's lights or not.

OUT OF LINE

Anytime you notice someone who is noticeably different from colleagues in actions or ideas, that person may be out of line without knowing it. At least two areas of activity could have spawned the expression.

A military line is not only expected to be as straight as an arrow, but each person in that line should move simultaneously.

Coordinated movement is also important in a chorus

dancing line. A single kicker who is a few seconds off can make the entire line look ragged.

Both of these activities are the possible beginnings for unacceptable ideas or behavior that peers judge inappropriate and that make anyone, anywhere, out of sync with the others in their group.

ROBOT

These days, you can hardly scroll on your feed without seeing a prediction that a robot powered by AI will soon be doing much of your work. Some who peer into the future may not realize that the name of the mechanical worker comes from the stage.

Karl Capek, a Czech playwright, was among the pioneers of modern science fiction. Capitalizing on publicity given to mechanical guns during World War I, he wrote a play called *R.U.R.*

The action of the drama centered on a group of mechanized monsters who revolted against their makers. Abbreviating the Czech term *robota*, meaning "work" or "drudgery," Capek called one of his imaginary machine men a "robot."

His play proved a tremendous hit. Few dramas of the 1920s provoked so much discussion. As a result, industrialized modern culture borrowed from the world of entertainment and many languages adopted the word. Today we even have the science of *robotics*.

CHAPTER 2

MANY WERE FAMOUS, OTHERS WERE RICH

S ometimes by means of their names, often as a result of their achievements, famous persons in every field have influenced our speech. So have others whose only claim to fame was wealth.

These stories are a far cry from the life and contributions of Bill Gates or the wealth of Jeff Bezos, but many of the words and expressions included here will be thriving long after these wealthy lifestyles have been lived.

Achilles' Heel
Amp
Best Foot Forward

ACHILLES' HEEL

Regardless of how tough a person may be, careful study will reveal a weak spot somewhere. Such was the case with one of the greatest legendary heroes of Greek mythology.

In ancient times it was common knowledge that the water of the river Styx was potent—so potent that a baby dipped into it received supernatural protection. Skin touched by the water remained pliable, but was as tough as steel.

One mother decided to give her son a kind of immortality. Hours after the boy was delivered, she hurried to the river and dipped him into the mysterious water. That made Achilles invulnerable over most of his body.

But in the end, Achilles was killed during the Trojan War by a wound in his heel—the part his mother held when she dipped him in the river. Water didn't touch his heel, so the mythological superman had a small but mortal flaw.

Stories about that warrior have survived after many centuries. As a result, any seemingly invincible person's weakest point is their Achilles' heel.

AMP

As a young teacher at the College de France, Andre Ampere made important discoveries about magnetism and electricity. His greatest achievement was highly technical: the discovery of fundamental properties of electrical currents.

Late in the 1880s, a world conclave of research scientists met in Paris. Probably because of Ampere's accomplishments and important discoveries, they decided to use his name as a label for a unit of electrical current.

In everyday use, the French surname was soon clipped in half. Now many a person can read a label and find out how many *amps* are used by an electrical appliance without needing to know how an ampere is measured.

BEST FOOT FORWARD

For a period of several centuries, European noblemen and wealthy gentry were greatly concerned about beauty. They affected ruffled sleeves, powdered wigs, black satin knee breeches, and full-length hose above buckled shoes.

Many of the idle rich were quite vain, and took pride in showing off a good pair of legs. Some went so far as to give preference to one leg as being more attractive than the other. Such a fellow wanted to make the greatest possible sensation at levees and balls. So he found a place where he could stand with his best-looking leg and foot in front, where it would attract many glances.

By the sixteenth century, a person wanting to make a good

impression knew just what to do. He put his "best foot for-ward," and by doing so helped to create a phrase we still use.

BLURB

American humorist Gelett Burgess, who was never more than a minute in any man's shadow, delighted readers and listeners of the 1890s. Some of his gags were so preposterous that at first they were taken seriously.

Poking fun at techniques used by advertisers, Burgess prepared a dummy book jacket for use at a publisher's convention. He stole a sketch of a lovely young woman and displayed it prominently. Beneath the picture he put a brief endorsement of the book by "Miss Belinda Blurb."

His prank was so successful that the humorist is credited with getting an artificial word into the English language single-handedly. Soon after Belinda Blurb's fake enthusiasm was circulated in 1907, any short but laudatory notice of a book, a record, a song, or a car came to be known as an *advertising blurb*.

BRAILLE

Every reader of Braille, along with most of us who don't have trained fingers, knows that the system of communicating by means of raised dots was devised by Louis Braille.

Born sighted, little Louis liked to play in his father's leatherworking shop. It was there that he was blinded by an awl at age three. His parents sent him to a special school, where he learned to recognize huge, embossed letters in books so big he could not lift them.

One day an army officer came to the school to demonstrate a system of raised dots and dashes. Since a message could be punched out in the dark, inventor Charles Barbier called his shorthand system *night writing*. Though Louis was only fifteen, his imagination was stoked. Within five years, he had improved and simplified the Barbier system. Braille's new unit of raised dots, three high and two wide, afforded sixty-two combinations.

It took decades for the system, worked out by a twenty-year-old, to win acceptance. Once it did, Braille dominated communication of the blind until use of audio equipment became widespread.

FREELANCE

Does your circle of acquaintances include a freelance artist or writer? Or maybe a musician or tax preparer? Whatever their field of activity may be, the modern freelancer is not on a payroll. Instead, services or products are offered directly to purchasers—often without a middleman.

The "lance" part of *freelance* harkens back to the Middle Ages when knights fought with sword and lance. Most warriors had sworn allegiance to the king or lord of their realm. Others were roving soldiers or medieval mercenaries who operated on their own, offering their swords, lances, and services to the highest bidder. *Freebooters* arose a few centuries later, and these fellows outfitted their own ships in order to prowl the seas. Today, we call them *pirates*.

The term *freelance* was popularized by the novel *Ivanhoe*, published in 1819. Oddly enough, the book was written by a knight, Sir Walter Scott. *Ivanhoe* brought to us a term that is more poetic and versatile than "self-employed person."

HIGH HORSE

When a friend's arrogance gets on your nerves, you may react with, "Get off your high horse!"

Long ago, a person's rank was mostly indicated by the steed they rode. Donkeys were used by peasants and serfs, and run-of-the-mill horses transported shopkeepers and petty gentry.

Big stallions bred and trained as chargers for use in tournaments and in war were reserved for the rich and famous. Before Columbus made his first voyage to the New World, England's pageants usually included at least one rider mounted on such a *charger*, or high horse. Today a person figuratively perched astride a big stallion is likely to be so pretentious that it calls for a rebuke.

PANDEMONIUM

Next time you find pandemonium breaking out around you, maybe you can shut out some of the noise by thinking of John Milton.

Why Milton, rather than another poet, novelist, or playwright? Because he's the indisputable father of the label we apply to "a chaotic uproar." Only a handful of persons have managed to coin a new word that has lasted. Milton was one of the few.

Writing of "the high Capital of Satan and his Peers" in his famous *Paradise Lost,* Milton combined the Greek words *pan* for "all" and *daimon* for "demon" into *Pandaemonium*—meaning literally "the place of all demons." His readers modified the spelling into today's more familiar form. Only a rare master of words could have thought of combining these five syllables in such rhythmic and evocative fashion.

SERENDIPITY

Maybe you made a simply terrific accidental discovery of some sort in the past. If not, one or several unforgettable experiences may lie ahead of you. For there's nothing quite like making a great find you didn't anticipate and toward which you didn't work.

Horace Walpole was already internationally famous when he wrote a 1754 letter in which this melodic word appeared for the first time. He'd been reading an ancient fairy tale from Ceylon, earlier called *The Three Princes of Serendip*. In the story, three legendary princes frequently stumbled across good things they did not anticipate.

The tales of Serendip so excited the imagination of Walpole that he told Sir Horace Mann about it. To the veteran British diplomat, his correspondent suggested that *serendipity* enables a person who's looking for one thing to find something else entirely.

Adopted by Walpole's literary followers, the made-up term filled a gap in language. Especially among scientists and inventors, serendipity has paid big dividends so often that the world would be a great deal poorer without its effects.

TYCOON

If given five seconds to name a modern tycoon, would you pick Bill Gates? Or does Warren Buffett seem a better choice for the title? Or perhaps you would think of Oprah Winfrey, one of America's wealthiest women.

Regardless of the financial or industrial tycoon who tops your personal list, that person has only one attribute of the tycoon of old. That quality is power—raw and undiluted.

The title we use so casually today was formed from Chinese words meaning "great prince." But the ancient Chinese never applied it to one of their own rulers. Instead, rivals located on a nearby island employed it when the Shogun of Japan was being described to foreigners.

All of which means that the modern tycoon, no matter how powerful their bankroll may be, doesn't quite sit on the throne occupied by a tycoon of old.

CHAPTER 3

FEATHERS AND FUR

Though they talk only in fables and fairy tales, birds and other animals have had wide and lasting impact upon our speech. Have domesticated creatures with features and furs influenced your everyday use of words more than wild ones? That's a tough question. Possibly these expressions will help you to answer it.

Buffalo
Chicken Feed
Dachshund
Eager Beaver
Feisty
Get One's Back Up
Greenhorn

Hightail
Jaywalker
Jinx
Mascot
Maverick
Raining Cats and Dogs

BUFFALO

Spanish conquerors of Mexico encountered an incredible animal in 1519. According to their description, the creature was "a rare Mexican bull, with crooked shoulders, a hump on its back like a camel and with hair like a lion."

Subsequent encounters with the "crooked-back ox" led amateurs to decide that it was kin to Asia's water buffalo. Naturalists rejected that idea and used *bison* to name the animal. They were too late to influence popular speech; many who flocked to the great American West hoped to get rich from "buffalo pelts."

Capable of galloping at forty-five miles per hour, the buffalo is the most ornery creature on the continent. Not only is the buffalo perpetually yearning for a fight, it is very hard to kill. It sometimes took sharpshooters on the prairie six attempts to stop a buffalo in its tracks.

This most distinctive of American beasts can also be the most frustrating. As a result, we say we are *buffaloed* by anything that leads to bewilderment, frustration, or helplessness.

CHICKEN FEED

Pioneers who moved into the American West took their domesticated animals with them. Chickens were high on the list of favorites because flocks could be fed through the winter on grain too poor for use in the kitchen.

Except for table scraps, inferior wheat and corn constituted the most common chicken feed. City dwellers picked up the farm-born expression and applied it to copper and silver coins.

By the time riverboat gambling became popular, the expression was being used to designate any small amount of money. One high-stakes gambler who cleaned out a novice complained that he had played all night for chicken feed—a meager $23.

DACHSHUND

German breeders developed an eccentric-looking dog with a slender body and tiny legs. It seemed only a curiosity until these features were found to be valuable. They gave the little creature built-in advantages as a hunter of the badger, or as the Germans called them, *dachs*. Prized by outdoor enthusiasts, the high-bred animal was known to them as the "badger hound," or *dachshund*.

Until recent times, breeders outside of Germany ignored the odd-looking animal. When they began to take interest, they treated it as an unusual pet rather than as a hunting dog. Nowadays, its distinctive build and good disposition have endeared it to hosts of owners, most of whom wouldn't know what to do with a badger if their low-slung hound should capture one.

EAGER BEAVER

If you plunge into a task or show enthusiasm, someone is likely to call you an *eager beaver*.

That title of admiration, says folklore, comes from watching colonies of beavers at work. Many pioneers swore that beavers started gnawing trees and slapping mud into crevices with their tales right after sunup. According to the same unimpeachable source, other beavers took their own sweet time about joining the dam-building gang.

Observation by biologists has demolished this myth. There's no such thing as a beaver who's spectacularly eager. All members of rodent colonies are more or less alike— hardworking and skilled, but not markedly different in pace.

That realization hasn't diminished the impact of the rhyming title. Often with admiration, it is applied to any two-footed animal who seems more than eager to get started.

FEISTY

Some persons, more or less lethargic by nature, hardly know how to make a comeback for a slight or a slur. Others, just the opposite, are so feisty that they seem to go about looking for opportunities to engage in spats and pick quarrels.

Members of the second category may not consider

themselves dogged, but if speech means anything, they're like some four-footed critters. For in the highly specialized language of the South Midland dialect, any quick-tempered lapdog is a *fice*.

At least in times past, the owner of a fice was likely to give it the best of food and a lot of attention. No wonder one of these pampered little animals was likely to have a temper with a short fuse!

Fice-like attitudes and reactions on the part of two-legged creatures warrant use of the label *feisty*—an indirect way of suggesting that a person is as snappy as a poodle.

GET ONE'S BACK UP

If a person or situation causes you to "get your back up," you're likely to behave at least a little like one of man's favorite animals. As recently as the end of the Middle Ages, no household was complete without a cat. Puss-in-Boots became an immortal literary figure during this period.

Few common sights are more impressive than that of a cat strutting about on its toes, with its back arched very high. This feline stance is so common that a human in a state of fury was compared with such an animal before Spain sent her armada against England in the end of the sixteenth century.

You may seldom or never make a noticeable change in the arch of your backbone. Nevertheless, when you show signs of rage or great indignation, your attitude is likely to cause you to be labeled with the expression that describes an angry cat.

GREENHORN

If you include a *greenhorn* in an activity at which you're an old pro, be on the alert for mistakes and be patient in correcting them!

Tender new leaves in the spring often seem to be a shade of green that is seen during no other season. Because such growth is young and fragile, anyone or anything lacking experience and strength came to be labeled as *green*.

Experienced handlers of oxen could identify awkward young males at a glance; their horns were small and unscarred. Such a greenhorn wasn't ready for a job that required stamina and training. Neither are most human adolescents or other newbies; though their heads have no bony protuberances, they are called by the name assigned to oxen with freshly sprouted horns.

HIGHTAIL

When you move at top speed, whether running on foot or driving a car, you hightail it from one place to another.

That is because early cowpokes noticed the actions of wild horses. Herds of them, descended from steeds of Spanish explorers, once roamed the West. Always, a stallion served as lookout for these animals; at the slightest sign of danger, he would signal for them to take off at top speed.

Domesticated horses follow the example of wild ones. When startled, they jerk their tails very high and burst into a gallop with a few strides. As a result of this equine trait, a person or vehicle getting off to a fast start is said to hightail it down the road.

JAYWALKER

Few North American birds are so loud and colorful as the blue jay. Now often seen in towns and suburbs of cities, the noisy creatures once avoided humans. Their prevalence in wooded regions caused any ruckus to be complained about and referred to as being "noisy as a jay bird."

Blue jays who ventured into urban areas often found themselves confused. Not understanding patterns of movement and ignorant of signs and caution lights, they seemed to endanger their lives when they flew across or landed on streets.

Based on this bird behavior, any erratic pedestrian seen in the city was referred to as being like a jay. Before long, *jaywalker* became the description of a person who crosses a street in a reckless or illegal fashion.

JINX

During a resurgence of interest in the occult, some people who didn't have much faith in horoscope readings went all out for fortune-telling by use of animals and birds.

One of the most popular of creatures for use in divination was the wryneck woodpecker—commonly known in much of the Southeast as "the jinx." Many a person who paid good money for information from a jinx regretted trying to peer into the future. Too often, none of the predicted good came about—while all the bad omens proved to be true.

This denouement was frequent enough to give the poor little woodpecker a bad reputation; disaster followed a reading by means of a jinx so often that the bird's name came to stand for bad luck.

MASCOT

French composer Edmond Audran was all but unknown until he produced a hit in 1880. Audiences in Paris applauded his *La Mascotte,* titled after a provincial word for a witch. The central character had such good luck that opera goers knew it had to come from supernatural sources.

Offered throughout Europe, the title of the opera came to label any object or person bringing good fortune. An early mascot might be a rabbit's foot or a four-leaf clover.

Gradually the vivid label was associated with animals and birds believed to bring luck. Schools, clubs, and sporting groups used them to represent their teams and bring good fortune. As a result, many an athlete who has never attended an opera trusts in the feathered or furry mascot that helps the team to win.

MAVERICK

Attorney Samuel A. Maverick migrated to Texas in the cowboy era of the early 1800s and built up a good practice. When one of his clients couldn't come up with cash, the newcomer from the east accepted some land in payment for his services. Soon he moved his herd to the Conquistar Ranch, near San Antonio.

Busy helping to fight Mexicans and win independence for Texas, the attorney spent little time on his ranch. Since he didn't check up on them, lazy hands did not bother to brand his calves. By the time he sold out in 1855, unbranded cattle were running all over the place.

Neighboring ranchers who came across one of Maverick's animals seldom hesitated to brand it and run it into one of their own herds. No one knows how many cattle the greenhorn rancher lost in this manner. But his name entered speech as a word for a nonconformist or malcontent who bears no signs of belonging to a specific herd.

RAINING CATS AND DOGS

If you're caught in a downpour, there is a good chance that you might hear someone say it's "raining cats and dogs."

These domesticated animals, and no others, are linked in speech with a furious storm. Some scholars think they know why. They point out that witches credited with causing storms often rode the winds in the form of black cats. And in Norse mythology, the god of storms was described as being surrounded by dogs plus their wild cousins, wolves.

Undocumented conjecture suggests that Norse mythology is the seedbed from which the modem phrase has grown. Another guess, equally plausible, is rooted closer to home.

Every furious gale, heard with a sensitive ear, sounds a lot like the sudden eruption of a dog-and-cat fight. Many householders used to keep half a dozen dogs and two or three cats. Perhaps comments that the "storm sounds just like cats fighting with the dogs" were turned into the metaphor crediting heavy clouds with raining cats and dogs.

CHAPTER 4

NAMES AND GAMES

Games, both athletic and not-so-athletic, have their special fascination. Part of it stems from the hope of winning—along with the fear of losing. Regardless of whether or not you've ever been a devotee, poker may have influenced your everyday vocabulary more profoundly than any other game. But other games have added to your everyday speech too.

Ace in the Hole
Back to Square One
Break the Ice
Dominoes
Draw the Line
Ducks in a Row
Jackpot

Off the Wall
On a Roll
Play for Keeps

ACE IN THE HOLE

Stud poker came into its own during the cowboy era. More than any other game, it separated cowpokes from their wages and miners from their dust. Complex rules govern the way in which cards are dealt, held, and played.

With other cards exposed so that opponents may see them, a lucky player sometimes holds an ace that is facedown—concealed "in the hole." That card may be the pivot on which a game turns.

Any asset or source of strength, kept secret by its holder, is so much like a concealed playing card that it is an ace in the hole.

BACK TO SQUARE ONE

Especially during a group activity, it is common for someone to propose a return to "square one." That is shorthand for suggesting: "Let's scrap all we've done, and start over."

Not a bad way to express the notion of giving up and making a fresh start, for the expression took shape during the pre-electronic era in which board games of many kinds were in use.

Several widely popular games involved moving tokens in response to throwing dice or drawing a card. At the beginning of a contest, all tokens were placed at the same starting point—square one of the board.

A proposal about "going back to square one" meant scrapping the ongoing game and starting a new one.

BREAK THE ICE

London, Leningrad, and many other great cities grew strong and important as a result of being situated on rivers and channels. This geographical advantage was worth little, however, in periods of bitter cold. Even large ships could become icebound, making them useless for weeks.

Small, sturdy ships known as *icebreakers* were developed to precede traveling ships and make a way through the ice. Such work was preliminary to the central task of transporting goods through freezing water.

Every veteran boatman knew that he often had to break the ice before actually getting down to business. Consequently the waterborne expression came to label any method of making a start.

DOMINOES

An Italian prisoner, forbidden to throw dice, may have been the inventor of a substitute game. It was played with twenty-eight pieces of wood, marked with spots representing all possible throws with two dice.

Soon devotees of the new game began making little tiles of ebony, covered with thin ivory. Such playing pieces reminded them of a special hood worn by priests. This heavy black garment, lined with white, was known as a *domino*.

After taking the name of the hood, "dice on tiles" swept through France and then across the channel into England. British players eventually used a plural form of the word, so *dominoes* became a favorite parlor game of the Edwardian era.

Most Americans have never seen a priest huddled in a domino, but many of them use English-style playing pieces that make dominoes a distant relative of shooting craps.

DRAW THE LINE

A game that was the ancestor of tennis involved hitting a ball back and forth across a net. It required little equipment, since players used their hands to strike the ball.

Precise dimensions for the court had not been established, so play could take place almost anywhere. Having selected a level spot, contestants stretched a net. Then each stepped an agreed distance from the net and drew a line that was the visual boundary.

For decades, players knocked balls back and forth in impromptu courts. Through influence of the game, the act of drawing a boundary line came to name the establishment of a limit of any kind.

DUCKS IN A ROW

Primitive versions of modern bowling were known many centuries ago. Pins of varied sizes and shapes were employed.

Eventually they were standardized at fifteen inches in both height and circumference.

Originally called "ten-pins," the equipment used in Europe was employed in the earliest American bowling saloons. The game was modified by the introduction of a short, slender pin that was compared with a duck and, by extension, called them "duckpins."

Players reset so many pins in rows that one who completes a task is commended as having put their "ducks in a row."

JACKPOT

Rare, indeed, is the person who wouldn't like to hit a jackpot of one variety or another. To many a casino patron, the jackpot is much like a hole in one is to a golfer—only more so, if possible.

A big payoff as a result of hard work and ingenuity—or luck at a slot machine—owes its name to an intricate form of poker. In draw-poker, a person must have a pair of jacks or better in order to open, but has to ante regardless. If no one holds such cards, the pot grows larger and larger. Sooner or later, someone will rake in a pile of chips by hitting the jackpot.

OFF THE WALL

Why do we sometimes say that a really unusual piece of art or a ridiculous plan is "off the wall?"

Because a wall is essential to several popular games, notably squash and handball. In these games, as well as in racquetball, a bounce from the wall is influenced by speed, spin, and angle. Even a veteran player cannot always estimate what direction a ball will take.

Like a ball bouncing at a weird angle, a plan or an activity may be so unpredictable that it, too, is described as being "off the wall."

ON A ROLL

Anytime you're congratulated as being "on a roll," you are seen as unbeatable for the moment. Such a winning streak, regardless of the field of activity involved, takes its name from gambling tables.

Every crapshooter, beginner or veteran, yearns for the time when each roll of the dice will produce another in a long string of wins. A first throw of seven or eleven signals that this may be the instant at which luck will start.

Lots of persons have either experienced this work of chance or watched others profit from it. Consequently, anyone enjoying a great streak of luck is lauded as being on a roll—even though tumbling a pair of dice may not be involved.

PLAY FOR KEEPS

Human nature being what it is, differences in personality often emerge very early. When marbles were high on the list of favorite toys for children, many bouts ended by sorting them out so everyone could go home with the ones that were brought.

But there was another, far more serious kind of play. Before starting it, opponents agreed that all marbles captured during competition would become the property of the winner. Any boy or girl who put a bag of marbles at risk was likely to have a little thicker skin than run-of-the-mill players—a competitor to be avoided by all except those also willing to play for keeps.

CHAPTER 5

SPORTS TALK OFTEN FOLLOWS THE BALL

Rough or gentle, so many sports involve the use of balls that conversation about them centers in many spheres of influence. Our indebtedness to sports is so great that you're "out in left field" if you never use expressions born from planned struggle.

Birdie
Caddy
Deadlock
Face-Off
Fall Guy
Game Plan
Pinch Hitter
Play the Field

Rodeo
Roll with the Punches
Tee
Throw in the Towel

BIRDIE

Admiration for native birds caused early Americans to use their name as a way of expressing commendation. Any admirable person was likely to be admired as a "bird."

Golfers who used *bogie* to name a score of one over par chose *birdie* to indicate one stroke under par. Coined in the United States, the term later spread to England and Europe.

In the 1953 Masters, Ben Hogan's ball lay sixty feet from the cup on the ninth hole. When he sank a birdie putt, it proved to be one of the decisive shots of the tournament. Playing the same course years earlier, James Demaret had scored six birdies in nine holes.

Regardless of the distance it covers, hearts beat faster when a birdie heads for the cup like a homing pigeon returning to its coop.

CADDY

Early golfers, some of whom were educated in France, were often assisted by *cadets*, or "young fellows," who carried their clubs. As the game matured, the label for a carrier of clubs became slurred in speech. Many a youth without a steady job was glad to work as a *caddy*.

That is how some golfing greats first walked the greens. Gene Sarazen was a caddy at Apawamis in Harrison, New York. John Byron Nelson, Jr., "the mechanical man" of the 1930s, earned seventy-five cents a round as a caddy at Glen Garden in Fort Worth. Ben Hogan started at sixty-five cents a round, plus tips.

Future players may never see a caddy except in cup competition. But in pre-mechanized days, a young fellow willing to carry bags was an essential ingredient to the elixir that is golf.

DEADLOCK

Wrestling was a highly developed sport at least five thousand years ago. Sculpture from temple tombs near the Nile indicate that ancient grapplers used many of the holds still in vogue.

No one knows precisely when the sport became prominent in Britain. But by the time noblemen became engrossed with chivalry, many commoners were wrestling fans.

It was not unusual for a burly yeoman to make a special move. A wrestler could hold someone indefinitely, even if he was unable to force a submission. Because it killed action, a hold of this sort was called a *deadlock*. Spreading from the ring, it came to label a stalemate of any kind.

FACE-OFF

Anticipating a confrontation and maybe hoping to avoid it, many a person has found themselves involved in a face-off.

This situation doesn't demand the presence of notables; it can develop between next-door neighbors or a pair of co-workers.

Chalk this expression up to sports, rather than meetings between world leaders.

As the start of a hockey game approaches, two players face one another tensed and poised. Each hopes to drive the puck when an official drops it between them. This hostile situation leads us to label any confrontation as a *face-off*.

FALL GUY

Late in the last century, professional wrestling made a sudden spurt in popularity. Grunt-and-groan men fanned out from metropolitan areas and scheduled matches in dozens of small cities, often at agricultural expositions and county fairs.

Many, if not most, of the matches were fixed. One wrestler would agree to take a fall for a stipulated sum. His opponent would promise to handle him gently. But in order to make a match look good, the winner was often quite rough with the fellow who took the fall.

In sporting circles, it became common to speak of a loser as a *fall guy*. Firmly fixed in American speech by 1900, the sports expression came to indicate any loser, victim, or dupe.

GAME PLAN

Pioneer football teams took to the field with nothing better than a general strategy to be used against all opponents. That was evidently the case with the Cumberland team that was beaten 220–0 by hard-driving, pass-throwing Georgia Tech.

Many teams experienced disasters that postgame analysis suggested they could have avoided. As a result, alert coaches began scouting their opponents in order to assess their style of play. In the light of such analysis, strategy was tailored to specific foes. That is, every upcoming clash evoked a planned pattern designed to make the most of an opposing team's weakness.

This technique worked so well in sports that business leaders adopted it. Now a charitable organization planning a fundraising campaign or a corporation about to launch a new product is almost certain to produce a detailed *game plan* long before the action begins.

PINCH HITTER

Every club and organization, along with practically all business enterprises, sometimes gets in a tight spot. Action is needed, and regular members of the team are reluctant to lead.

Regardless of the nature of the near-crisis, the situation calls for a pinch hitter—someone with highly specialized skills who will not be expected to do more than use those skills briefly.

In baseball, that describes the function of a substitute batter, called to the plate late in the game with runners on base. He may be awkward in the field and unable to throw anything but a slow, straight ball, but he is amazing with a bat.

Many situations have demanded pinch hitters for special tasks. As a result, the baseball term is applied to anyone called on to substitute for an entertainer or speaker who fails to make it to the "plate" as scheduled.

PLAY THE FIELD

Horse racing, "the sport of kings," attracts people willing to take a risk. Anyone wanting some of the action, confident they've picked a winner, is likely to bet on only one animal.

Those less sure or more cautious like to spread both risk and opportunity. Often that means placing a wager on half the horses in a race. With luck, winnings will be larger than losses when money is spread throughout the field.

Such action in the realm of romantic relationships can be even more risky—and potentially more rewarding—than choices made at the betting window. Here, too, some are bold enough to concentrate on a sure thing, while others "play the field" in order to hedge their bets.

RODEO

At roundup time, cowboys of the Old West staged impromptu sporting events. In 1882 a Pecos, Texas, rancher offered $100 prizes in bronco riding, bulldogging, and roping. Yet these contests had no formal name until 1916. That is when a promoter turned to Spanish for "roundup" and sold tickets to his *rodeo*.

As a money-making sport, rodeo spread throughout the

world. By the time it reached Madison Square Garden in the 1940s, prize money amounted to nearly $100,000.

Today, a rodeo still rounds up big crowds.

ROLL WITH THE PUNCHES

There is no way to go through life without being on the receiving end of a lot of punches. But you can try to deal with them as a skillful boxer does.

A beginner in the ring may try to slug it out with an opponent, hoping to catch sight of a haymaker in advance and dodge it. Many veterans insist that it is useless to try to avoid blows. Far better, they say, to reduce impact by bending or stepping to reduce the impact of an oncoming padded fist.

So if you adopt a pattern of rolling with life's punches, you'll find you can take a lot of punishment without going down for the count.

TEE

From an old Scottish term, a wee pile of earth pulled together by a golfer or his caddy came to be called a *tee*. Little mounds of dirt eventually gave way to wooden tee-pegs that were whittled by hand and valued because they lifted balls rather than cushioned them.

Few pioneer clubs had rules governing the size of a tee. Many early players had elaborate ones they prized so highly that they tried to avoid breaking or losing them. Only with the advent of hard rubber and plastic has the tee become throw-away equipment.

Unique as a piece of sporting gear, the tee has spawned a vocabulary of its own. A person can "tee off"—make a start—in a business venture or "tee up" the next presenter in a meeting as well as on the first hole.

THROW IN THE TOWEL

Before anyone thought of calling pugilism a science, sluggers went at one another helter-skelter. Even after bare fists were abandoned in favor of light gloves, victory was usually won by strength rather than skill.

Many bruised and battered fighters found they could not get to their feet when they heard the signal for a new round to begin. Handlers of such a fighter knew that there was nothing to do but give up. So one of them would toss into the ring an article used to soak up blood—a towel.

Modern boxing is replete with rules designed to outlaw the brutality of the past. Even the lingo of the ring has become larger and richer. But in an era of instant replays for television, a person forced to give up at ringside or anywhere else is still said to *throw in the towel*.

CHAPTER 6

THESE MAKE SENSE

Many of our everyday words and phrases make complete sense; they point to events and activities that are familiar and readily understood. Their development has been logical and orderly. Yet most of them have additional meanings that we employ without a thought because they are so familiar.

AWOL
Backlog
Brainstorming
Disguise
Make the Grade
Moonlight
Olive Branch
Out of Touch
Read Between the Lines
Rub the Wrong Way

AWOL

These days, it's possible for one of your fellow workers to go *AWOL* or walk off the job without giving notice. Earlier, this form of conduct was limited to members of the military.

A servicemember wearing the uniform of their country's army or navy or marine corps was never under any delusions about what they could and couldn't do. Discipline is basic to military life.

But many a buck private in the rear rank or brand-new member of a ship's crew simply walked off their base or vessel when the notion struck them. When discovered and placed under arrest—as they almost always were, sooner or later—they were listed on the roster as having been "absent without official leave."

The initial letters of the damning record, A.W.O.L., became the brand-new word, *AWOL*.

BACKLOG

Pioneers faced a serious problem when it came to finding fire sources. Matches were rare, and flint and steel often failed in damp weather. So many pioneers tried to keep a fire burning without interruption for months at a time.

A big green log, next to stones in the back of a fireplace, would smolder for days. Dry wood would be laid in front of it to burn, and the next morning the backlog yielded embers from which a new blaze could be started.

As a rule, the backlog was not used for fuel, although it

could be pulled out and burned in an emergency. Today we call any sort of reserve a *backlog*.

BRAINSTORMING

Anytime you come up with a really new idea, it may be the product of individual or group brainstorming.

F. W. H. Myers, a distinguished leader of investigators, founded the Society for Psychical Research in 1882. His movement soon became the talk of the Western world. With initial study coming to focus upon telepathy, editors compared it with radio and suggested that brain waves made it possible. Engineers already knew that electrical storms affect many types of communication. That made it an easy step to compare a radio that acted strangely with an electrical storm in the brain.

Still far from understanding such states, we know that brain activity somehow fosters creativity and spontaneity. Which explains why *brainstorming* is regularly sponsored by some of our biggest research laboratories and corporations.

DISGUISE

For four hundred years after the fall of Rome, Europe was in turmoil. When stable political patterns were formed, rulers demanded strict conformity. Written and oral codes eventually prescribed every detail of a person's *guise*, or dress. Color, shape, and material of a guise indicated occupation, rank, and place of residence.

Nefarious medieval characters saw a golden opportunity to assume false positions. By putting on appropriate clothing and going to a strange district, a sharp-witted person could pose as a goldsmith, physician, monk, or even a knight.

By 1350 imposters in false guise were so common that any masquerade came to be known as a *disguise*. Few persons adopted such an outfit unless they wished to become imposters or perpetrate hoaxes. Hence the venerable label took on sinister connotations still taken for granted except on Halloween.

MAKE THE GRADE

When you succeed in fundraising or mastery of a new golf course, you *make the grade*.

US railroads had only forty miles of track in 1830. Expanding from that base, engineers found that the pulling power of an iron horse is greatly affected by the slope, or grade, of a track. When a train moves from a level section to a 1 percent grade, five times as much steam is needed.

A grade of 3 percent or more challenged the power of locomotives and called for a celebration when the top was reached. Hence anyone who overcame obstacles of any kind was lauded by railroaders as having "made the grade."

MOONLIGHT

These days many people decide to moonlight by holding down a second job in addition to a first one. Few descriptive terms are more appropriate than this one.

Its birth coincided with the advent of the forty-hour work week. Many employees accustomed to a fifty-six-hour week hardly knew what to do with the extra time; besides, they needed additional money.

Night afforded lots of opportunities to take on a second job, usually part-time. Now that industries and businesses operate around the clock, lots of people working a second or third shift moonlight in broad daylight. Nowadays *moonlighting* can also refer to a side gig or side hustle.

OLIVE BRANCH

Egyptians began experimenting with a native shrub at least four thousand years ago. Soon they produced varieties that yielded fine oil from the shrub's fruit. As a result, the olive came into cultivation around the entire Mediterranean basin.

In the biblical story of the great deluge, a freshly plucked olive branch was the first thing to give hope to Noah and his shipmates. Soon this harbinger of good tidings was followed by a promise that the flood would never be repeated.

As a result of that memorable incident, an olive branch became a symbol of peace and goodwill. Even in lands far too cold for the evergreen tree with edible fruit, the expression born in Egypt is almost universally understood.

OUT OF TOUCH

Late in the eighteenth century, many European military leaders moved toward use of tighter formations. Men were required to maintain rigid patterns even when on the march. As a practical way of regulating his space, the soldier in the ranks had to be sure that his swinging elbows would touch those of comrades on each side.

Whenever there was a gap in a line, it meant that some man was literally out of touch. Civilians adopted the military term and expanded its meaning to indicate any situation in which a person has (almost always figuratively) lost contact.

READ BETWEEN THE LINES

Simple methods of writing in code were devised long ago. Both Julius Caesar and Charlemagne sent battle reports in cipher. But the rise of cryptography as a scientific study dates from the sixteenth century.

Rulers, diplomats, military leaders, and business executives adopted the practice of writing in code. Some personal papers of England's Charles I, who ruled in the first half of the seventeenth century, were so obscure that they were not deciphered until about 1850.

To a person ignorant of the code, a secret paper was meaningless. Ordinary folk fascinated with this mystery concluded that the meaning was not in lines of gibberish, but in the space between them. Writing between lines with invisible ink strengthened this notion.

Except among intelligence agencies, interest in secret writing eventually waned. But language had already been enriched. Spawned from literal views of cryptographs, reading between the lines came to suggest the finding of inferences in any document.

RUB THE WRONG WAY

If you are sensitive, it may not take much to "rub you the wrong way." A thoughtless remark, a challenging look, or inattention to what you just said may be enough to do the trick.

Long ago, it took a different set of actions to spawn the expression.

Wealthy ladies of the colonial era were proud of their wide-board oak floors. At least once a week, servants wet-rubbed and then dry-rubbed surfaces. Though simple and routine, these tasks involved running mops along the grain of the wood. A careless worker sometimes mopped across the grain, producing streaks on the floor. To that worker's mistress, such cleaning was worse than none.

Vexation at a domestic worker who rubbed the wrong way was common enough to cause the housekeeping phrase to label clumsy or inept dealings with people as well as with floors.

CHAPTER 7

WORDS FROM AFAR

Many words and phrases are naturalized citizens, born and reared far from the streams of speech that produced the English language. Some have been polished so smoothly by frequent use that they aren't immediately recognized as having come from a great distance. Were they not in our working vocabularies, everyday speech would be less colorful and precise.

Alibi
Atlas
Blue Jeans
Character
Cologne
Guru
Junk
Panic

Shampoo
Taboo

ALIBI

Courtroom practices are slow to change. Lawyers continued to use Latin long after it was abandoned in everyday speech.

A Latin term meaning "elsewhere" was standard in criminal cases for centuries. Many a defense attorney rested her case upon evidence that her client was *alibi* at the time of the crime.

Use of the centuries-old term was so common that it entered modern speech with no change in spelling and little in meaning. An accused person who is able to establish an *alibi* is almost like a citizen in the realm of the Caesars who answered an accusation by saying they were elsewhere when the deed was done.

ATLAS

Anytime you make detailed plans for a trip, you are likely to seek information from an atlas—using a volume whose name has traveled a long way through both space and time.

Greek mythology described Atlas, once one of the Titans who ruled the universe, as holding a flat earth upon his shoulders. Had he not held it firmly, verbal lore insisted, travel would have been impossible upon a vibrating earth. That idea caused geographers of later centuries to dedicate published collections of maps to the titan who made travel possible.

With capitalization dropped and earth-bearing Altas largely forgotten, the name of the imaginary figure from the past now designates any book consisting primarily of maps.

BLUE JEANS

Many European cities once specialized in making a distinctive cloth of some kind. Heavy twilled cotton from Janua (modern Genoa) was called *jean* after its point of origin. In 1495, King Henry VII of England bought 262 bolts of it. *Jeans*, or male garments made from jean, were prized because they didn't wear out quickly.

Undyed fabric was used for generations before a batch of cloth dyed blue was turned over to cutters and sewers. The resulting blue jeans quickly made undyed ones obsolete.

CHARACTER

Metal workers of classical Greece developed a special tool used in marking. In time, such a *character*, or instrument—whose name was altered in passing through several languages— came to designate any mark made by it.

Medieval courts made much use of characters. Convicted of murder, a person given penal servitude instead of the gallows was branded with the character "M." In the same fashion, an arsonist's forehead or shoulder bore the character "A."

Anyone branded by authorities was marked for life. One glance at a character told a stranger what offense had been committed. As a result, the term indicating a branded letter came to stand for the sum total of a person's moral qualities.

COLOGNE

Do you prefer to whiff cologne rather than the heavier scent of perfume?

Pure air helped persuade the Roman emperor Claudius to choose a special site for a city. Named the "Colonia Agrippina" in honor of his wife, the place flourished. By the time it had become a beautiful German city of cathedrals, it was known as *Cologne* in England and France, and *Köln* in Germany.

An Italian merchant who lived there learned to make a light scent by adding alcohol and aromatic oils to traditional perfume bases. His Cologne water, or *eau de Cologne*, prompted dozens and then hundreds of perfumers to adapt his technique.

GURU

Regardless of how you earn your living, it's likely there is at least one nationally recognized guru in your field.

Why do these experts receive a centuries-old title from India? In that ancient land, it takes a lot of living for a person to become venerable—or *guru*. Many gurus proved to be charismatic leaders who attracted wide followings, and most were seemingly ageless. More interested in leadership skills than in age, we adopted the title and applied it to any outstanding authority.

JUNK

An early Asian sailing vessel, or *junk*, had a flat bottom and high poop deck that made it clumsy in heavy seas. What's more, one of these crafts was likely to be loaded up the sides with items no seasoned sailor would accept as a gift. Such strange and apparently useless cargo came to bear the name of the ship that transported it.

Junks were long ago replaced by steamers, generally Western in design. Their name lives, however, as a label for any accumulation of worn-out and cast-off clothing, furniture, tools, auto parts, or other gear.

PANIC

Severe or mild panic is brought about by sudden mounting fear. Whatever its level, the panic perpetuates an ancient notion that something was wrong and might get worse.

Unusual sounds heard in the forest by Greeks were attributed to their god Pan. He was believed to be very mischievous and playful as the god of forests, animals, and nature in general. Noises attributed to him produced a special kind of breathless apprehension that Greeks called *panic fear*.

Our name for sudden and overwhelming terror has survived for centuries after Pan ceased to be a special source of fear.

SHAMPOO

Early travelers in India were intrigued by a native custom. Sultans and *nabobs* had special servants who massaged their bodies after hot baths. From a native term for "to press," such a going-over of the body with knuckles was called a *champo*, or *shampoo*.

Europeans were skeptical of its merits and sometimes afraid. One explorer said he wouldn't have taken the risk had he not seen several Chinese merchants shampooed before his turn came.

Outnumbered by a ratio of 40,000:1, every outsider—from merchant prince to soldier—learned to enjoy the luxury of a daily shampoo by servants.

Taken to England, the invigorating ritual quickly shrank to nearly nothing. Only the wealthy could afford to keep a professional bath attendant on the household staff. So by 1860, the once-exotic term of washing and rubbing only referred to cleaning the scalp—usually without help.

TABOO

Europeans who ventured into the South Seas during early voyages of exploration were intrigued by colorful native customs. Some of the most puzzling were those that forbade passage or contact.

Among the Tongans, it seemed that everywhere a sailor turned, they were confronted by a priest who barred their way and muttered: "Tabu! Tabu!" (Forbidden! Forbidden!) No forbidden object could be touched, or even examined from a distance, and a forbidden place could not be entered.

Famous explorer Captain Cook and other sailors altered

the Polynesian term a trifle and returned home with the novel sound that expressed warning. Several classical and European words indicating caution were supplanted by the novel expression from the South Seas.

As a result, to speakers of numerous modem languages, anything forbidden is now likely to be termed *taboo*.

CHAPTER 8

MONEY, BUSINESS, AND COMMERCE

B usiness, flowing by exchange of money, doesn't tolerate foolishness. Therefore it would seem logical that the vocabulary of commerce would be straightforward and forthright, devoid of imagination. Not so. As in other fields of endeavor, commerce borrows freely from any available source in order to form or to enrich a word or a phrase. Conversely, everyday speech often owes money and business a debt not noticed at a casual glance.

Cold Feet
Dollar
Diddly-Squat
Fiasco
Loophole

Make Ends Meet
Off the Cuff
Phony
Selling Like Hotcakes
Silhouette

COLD FEET

In rural Europe, a person with little money—hence unwilling to move toward a purchase—was often described as having "cold feet." A gambler wanting out of a game could let it be known that he was dead broke by saying that his feet were cold.

With its fiscal roots forgotten, the ancient expression remains alive and well. Regardless of whether they're pursuing a sweetheart or planning to change jobs, a person who suddenly withdraws from the action is labeled as having *cold feet*.

DOLLAR

A silver mine opened in Bohemia in 1516 turned out to be one of the richest ever. So much precious metal was dug out that local jewelers couldn't use all of it. As a result, craftsmen made one-ounce coins from some of the silver.

In commerce the novel coin soon became familiar as the *thaler*. So many thalers were circulated that the product of Bohemia became a standard unit of currency. English merchants eager for international deals stumbled over the name of the silver piece and wound up calling it "dollar." Dollars soon poured into and out of the island kingdom, but the coin was never made official.

Patriots who shaped our 1785 American monetary system wanted to be completely un-English. They devised a decimal system quite unlike that which made a guinea worth twenty-one shillings. Founding fathers scrapped both "pound" and "penny" and chose *dollar* to name a piece worth one hundred cents.

DIDDLY-SQUAT

Sometimes a person has no opinion or feeling about an issue. Asked to take a pro or con stance, Andy Griffith might well respond: "I don't care diddly-squat; it makes no difference to me."

Strictly American in origin, that expression sounds suspiciously like a pair of modified barnyard terms—but isn't.

Carnival workers who traveled from town to town working one county fair after another developed their own private language. They had to do so in order to attract potential people who would pay for a chance at a cheap prize. *Diddle-e-squat* seems to have entered carnival talk to name "money"—often a nickel or a dime, since that was the going rate for a game of chance.

Frequently used to hide talk about a small amount of money, it was an easy and natural transition for the carnival term to indicate very little of anything.

FIASCO

Long ago, Venice became a great center of the glass trade. Venetian craftsmen developed the now-standard goblet made up of bowl, stem, and foot. They also imitated semiprecious stones in the color and texture of fine ware. Many pieces were so prized that royal inventories listed them along with gold and silver vessels.

In addition to costly ware, Italian artisans produced great quantities of the common flask—which in some dialects was known as a *fiasco*.

Flaws frequently developed in the process of turning out fine pieces. Glass was too expensive to throw away; even damaged, a hunk of it could be reheated and turned into a fiasco or two. So many inexpensive flasks were the result of bungling that the glass blower's term came to indicate any type of failure.

At least, that is maybe the most believable of half a dozen theories offered to account for the rise of a distinctive and elusive word.

LOOPHOLE

If you find a loophole in a contract or an insurance policy, it will constitute an escape route for one of the parties. This usage stems from a turnabout in understanding of the name for what was once a special kind of tangible hole.

During the Middle Ages, architects and builders had to deal with the matter of defending a castle, once it was erected.

Longbows, followed by crossbows, were formidable weapons typically used by both attackers and defenders. A narrow window, often oval at the top and wider at the inner side of a thick wall, was found to offer a difficult target from across a moat. At the same time, such an opening was big enough to enable defenders to fire at will.

This special form of loophole saved the hide of many a lord of the manor. When firearms made it obsolete, its name transferred to any opening that provides an advantage to one party in a dispute or an agreement.

MAKE ENDS MEET

Full-rigged sailing vessels were equipped with a number of masts, each of which bore several sails. Since most pieces of canvas were raised and lowered separately, rigging involved hundreds of ropes. Many of these were movable, so were easily repaired when they broke.

Some ropes attached to lower edges of sails were permanently fixed. When such a length of hemp broke, frugal masters ordered sailors to pull ends together and splice them. In order to make both ends of a fixed rope meet, it was often necessary to strain and tug, stretching a piece of canvas to its limit.

Long used literally on the sea, we now apply the expression for "succeeding with difficulty" to anyone who makes both ends meet by managing to stretch their income to cover all bills.

OFF THE CUFF

The internet now makes it difficult for anyone to treat debts casually. If a person has an outstanding obligation, a quick search is likely to reveal it. Today's transactions are a far cry from what they were a few generations ago.

So is easy credit. As late as the era of Theodore Roosevelt, many merchants seldom let people get merchandise without putting cash on the barrel head. Credit was so limited that a fellow operating a livery stable could keep his records on his shirt cuff.

Which meant that a drifter who lived "on the cuff" was adept at talking folk into extending credit without formality. Casual business transactions were common enough to cause anything impromptu to be termed "off the cuff."

PHONY

When you say that a piece of jewelry or a work of art is *phony*, you owe the label to early Irish scammers. One of the favorite ruses of those swindlers was the "fawney rig"—given that name from Irish for a "finger-ring."

A con artist using this stratagem put a ring, or fawney, in a public place. Sooner or later someone would come along and pick up the piece equipped with an imitation stone. Appearing from nowhere, the swindler persuaded or frightened his victim into paying him to keep quiet about the find. Making off with hush money, the con man would leave the sucker holding a fawney that seemed valuable but was actually worthless.

So many people were defrauded that anything fake came to be called *fawney*. The original Irish word was *fáinne*, in England it became *fawney*, and it was finally Americanized to *phony*.

SELLING LIKE HOTCAKES

Newcomers to North America found one of its most versatile plants to be Indian corn, or *maize*. When dried and ground, corn yielded meal that made fine bread.

An unknown experimenter discovered still another use for cornmeal: when batter fried on a griddle, a cake made of cornmeal yielded a fluffy delicacy that was best while still hot. Homesteaders said they preferred their hotcakes fried in bear grease, but town folk were partial to pork lard.

Whenever a Ladies' Aid Society put on a benefit, cooks found it hard to keep up with the demand for hotcakes. Their popularity and money-raising power was so great that by 1825, any merchandise that moved in a hurry was described as "selling like hotcakes."

SILHOUETTE

Any time you see a silhouette, the stark appearance of the black outline can serve as a reminder that its name was bestowed in mockery of a penny-pincher.

Étienne de Silhouette became controller-general of France in 1759. Selected because he was considered capable of solving the nation's financial troubles, he went to work with zeal. All of his money-saving proposals were unpopular, but his suggestion that government pensioners receive reduced allowances created a national uproar.

For generations, street artists had offered outline portraits at low prices. Since these represented an extreme example of economy in art, ridicule of the financier caused his name to become attached to them.

CHAPTER 9

WHY DON'T FOLKS SAY
PRECISELY WHAT THEY MEAN?

The author of *Dr. Jekyll and Mr. Hyde*, Robert Louis Stevenson, lived long before modern scientific study of communication. But from personal experience, he knew that a listener or reader has to interpret what they hear. That process is usually so easy that it is automatic. But many a word and phrase seems on the surface to suggest something quite different from original connotations or the meaning found by "a willing and prepared hearer."

Beat Around the Bush
Bitter Pill to Swallow
Carry a Torch
Kick the Bucket
Lay an Egg

BEAT AROUND THE BUSH

Noblemen and gentry who went in for the sport of boar hunting were glad for others to do the dangerous work. So they employed young males who fanned out through woods and swamps, making noise in order to beat animals toward the hunters.

The razor-sharp teeth of a big boar were lethal weapons no one wanted to encounter. Unarmed beaters frequently stayed out of dense clumps of undergrowth where a boar might be hiding. So many of them beat around the bush instead of going through it that their tactic came to label any evasive technique.

BITTER PILL TO SWALLOW

Any unpleasant news may be called "a bitter pill to swallow." Figuratively applied to a wide range of situations, the expression was once painfully literal.

For centuries, a physician's pellet for use in sickness has been known as a *pill.* Honey and spices were about all that doctors had to try to mask disagreeable components. Bark of a New World tree, the *cinchona*, was effective in fighting malaria. But the quinine it contains is extremely bitter.

Widely employed in the era before medications were coated, cinchona pellets caused any disagreeable thing to be termed "a bitter pill to swallow."

CARRY A TORCH

Torchlight parades were common features of political campaigns in rural America. Accompanied by drums or other musical instruments, an evening demonstration was likely to be loud and colorful.

Only enthusiastic followers took part in such rallies. A fellow who carried a torch didn't care who knew that he was wholeheartedly behind his candidate.

It was an easy transition to move from describing a passionate political follower to speaking of an ardent lover. These days, many will carry a torch for someone not interested in winning a political office.

KICK THE BUCKET

Until recent times, most slaughter of meat animals took place on the farm. Swine, sheep, and goats were comparatively easy to handle. But not a steer that weighed one-half ton or more.

A special hoist was devised for use with heavy animals. With its hind feet tied to a rope, a steer or an ox was pulled toward a beam at the top of a three-legged frame. A heavy wooden cask or bucket was shoved under the animal to prevent waste.

Frequently the rope was jerked as pullers strained to get

a carcass into position. This action threw the feet of the animal against the bucket, almost as though it were deliberately kicking.

By the time a steer or a prize hog kicked the bucket, its throat had already been slit. Consequently the farm expression came into use to name death in any form.

LAY AN EGG

Did your sports team ever "lay an egg"? Chances are that it did.

That expression sounds complimentary. When a barnyard fowl produces an egg, the critter is appreciated for its achievement. Not so in the human world, especially the realm of sports.

In the game of cricket, you score a "duck's egg" if you have no runs at bat because an egg resembles the shape of a zero. What better way to express the notion of "no score" than to say a team laid a duck egg or a goose egg?

It is no longer necessary to make zero points in order to *lay an egg*. Any significant failure may evoke the expression that was once highly descriptive and self-explanatory.

LET THE CAT OUT OF THE BAG

British tenants who farmed land belonging to gentry were supposed to turn over part of all they produced as rent. Many adhered to the letter of the law, but some sold suckling pigs, considered a delicacy and easily carried, without reporting the transactions. Frequently concealed in bags while being taken to market, black market animals were bought by butchers at bargain prices.

By the eighteenth century, shrewd farmers had learned that in a hasty illegal sale, it was easy to pass off a cat as a young pig. When a suspicious buyer insisted on seeing the merchandise before he paid, he sometimes found his doubts confirmed.

Today, a person with inside information may slip and give clues. Even though neither a feline nor a bag is involved, comrades are likely to chide the revealer of the secret for having "let the cat out of the bag." And a person who makes a hasty purchase without taking a look at merchandise is still said to have bought a "pig in a poke."

NOSE FOR TROUBLE

As noses go, those of most humans are second- or third-rate. Many wild animals depend on their sense of smell for much information about the outside world, as do most breeds of dogs. But for typical persons, the nose is simply an air vent in which organs of smell are located deep inside. Range of sensitivity to odors is extremely wide. Some people react readily to scents that others cannot detect by deliberate effort.

Capacity to anticipate the coming of unpleasant events is an equally big variable. Unable to explain special sensitivity in this arena, common folk quipped that it must be due to keenness of smell. As a result, anyone regarded as having special ability to detect impending problems is admired as having "a nose for trouble."

PULL A FAST ONE

Should someone try to pull a fast one on you, take charge. Look at details carefully and insist that sales talk or shuffled papers be slowed down. If you don't, there is a good chance you will lose. That is probably what happened many times during or soon after the 1920s.

Many an obscure baseball pitcher seemed mediocre until a moment of crisis. That's when he would pull a fast one—hurling a ball at such speed that the batter would be caught off guard. Another deception centered on movements of a dancer. Using a confederate, or shill, many a scammer shuffled clumsily for maybe ten or fifteen minutes. When onlookers were persuaded to wager about his skill, he would pull a fast one. That is, he would move his feet so fast it was impossible to follow them.

Emulating the baseball pitcher who suddenly develops blistering speed, and maybe the shuffle dancer as well, there are folks who will try to pull a fast one—or get away with a smooth swindle—in almost every area of activity.

SIDEBURNS

Civil War General Ambrose E. Burnside was almost as dashing a figure as was George Armstrong Custer. In most public appearances, he sported a hat so flamboyant that it took his name. Defying established custom, Burnside shaved his chin smooth while displaying a full mustache and side bar whiskers.

Thousands of men wore Burnside hats and adopted the Burnside style of facial hair. But reversal of syllables is a common form of word play. Many a dashing fellow who prided himself on his lovely burnsides enjoyed turning the name around. Inverted in popular speech, whiskers that imitated those of the general's became *sideburns*.

The vogue for side whiskers has waxed and waned. Since then, the colorful name adapted from that of a general has been used to designate any patch of hair in front of a man's ears.

CHAPTER 10

THE GREAT OUTDOORS

Our ancestors lived much more of their lives outside than we do. They took many colorful examples from nature and passed on to us a linguistic heritage rich in references to the great outdoors.

Ballpark Estimate
Bark up the Wrong Tree
Field Day
Get a Rise
Horseplay
On Cloud Nine
Out on a Limb
Play hooky
Through the Grapevine
Thunderstruck

BALLPARK ESTIMATE

When you talk to your accountant about the bottom line on your tax return, you want an exact figure—not a ballpark estimate.

In the days when all baseball games were played in the open air during daylight hours, journalists would have liked to know precisely how many fans showed up for a given game. But they seldom found out because owners and managers were cagey, and it was hard to get a precise head count. Besides, publicity about a low turnout might keep people away from the next game.

It became standard practice to give a very broad estimate—plus or minus a few hundred or a few thousand—when asked about the size of the gate on Saturday afternoon. Influence of what has long been billed as "America's national pastime" made the *ballpark estimate* our standard label for any rough count.

BARK UP THE WRONG TREE

Early European settlers in the United States discovered a new prey for hunting. Raccoons and possums were abundant, and could be hunted with nearly any kind of dog. When first pursued, a racoon would run through the underbrush. But as dogs neared, the animal would climb the nearest tree. Barking and jumping underneath, dogs tried to keep their quarry at bay until hunters came to make the kill.

Sometimes, however, a shrewd animal played a trick.

After climbing a tree, it worked its way through branches and across other trees to freedom—leaving dogs barking under an empty tree. This outcome of a hunting expedition was common enough to cause us to say another person is mistaken by commenting they are "barking up the wrong tree."

FIELD DAY

Once in a while everyone ought to enjoy a field day. It makes no difference *what* you do; romping around and having things pretty much as you want them is a special kind of self-rewarding activity.

That is what members of fraternities, sororities, and civic clubs discovered long ago. Instead of sticking strictly to routine, many groups of this nature would announce that two weeks from Saturday, every member would spend the day outdoors. Rivals were challenged to set the day aside, too, in order to compete in games and sports.

Canny leaders often arranged things so that it would be difficult or impossible for a tough set of opponents to be on hand at the time selected. This meant that sponsors could cavort through the field day, having things their own way and gloating at winning easy victories.

GET A RISE

Sometimes a casual comment from you will get a rise from a listener. A quick retort may run the gamut from minor vexation to high-level indignation. Whatever the response, if it is accompanied by reddening of the face and neck, you may be sure you have hit a tender spot.

But you don't have to be fishing for a heated comeback in order to get one. It can be triggered by a perfectly innocent remark.

Rapidity of response in such a situation is similar to a hungry fish rising to the bait. A human whose emotions are aroused by a sentence, a phrase, or even a single word rises to it like a bass going for a fly.

HORSEPLAY

During many centuries, horses were rare and expensive. Some knights actually did dash about Europe on spirited chargers. But oxen and donkeys were the most abundant and familiar beasts of burden.

Rarity of horses meant that it was quite an experience to see one of them frisking about a field or wallowing in dust. A big animal who lay on its back with all four feet flailing was obviously having a good time. So was a pasture mate who ran up to another in order to nuzzle.

Rough wallowing of a stallion and gentler romping of a mare was compared with boisterous action of humans. As a result, since the sixteenth century we have used *horseplay* to label rowdy and prankish behavior—indoors as well as outdoors.

ON CLOUD NINE

Before the advent of adding machines and calculators, even simple arithmetic was difficult. People forced to wrestle with multiplication and division developed special admiration for the number nine, believing it was the most powerful single-digit number.

This view may have been a byproduct of reverence for the Holy Trinity, since nine is three times three. As late as the Victorian Age, a person sporting the finest possible outfit was often described as being "dressed to the nines." Tradition having asserted that clouds exist in a series of successively higher layers, it was logical to label the ultimate height as *cloud nine*.

A victorious contestant or a person suddenly made exuberant seems literally to be soaring in the clouds. Naturally, therefore, someone who hits the ultimate joy is still likely to say, "I'm on cloud nine!"

OUT ON A LIMB

A person who finds themselves "out on a limb" is in a precarious position, with no sure or easy way to get out of the predicament.

That is precisely the situation of a possum or raccoon who takes to a tree and misjudges the distance to another. Having moved far out on a limb in order to jump to safety, such an animal suddenly realizes that there is no escape from its pursuer. It is too far to jump, and dogs are already under the tree, barking to bring hunters for the kill.

Though barely a century old in literary use, the hunting term born on the American frontier may have been used as early as colonial times.

PLAY HOOKY

Isaak Walton, one of the most widely read early writers about fishing, stressed the importance of getting the hook fixed firmly in the mouth of a fighting fish. His followers, conscious that this required a sudden jerk of the line, began to use *hook* as a verb of action. A person who decamped hastily was said to "hook it"; Charles Dickens used the phrase in this sense.

Compulsory education gave some youngsters an incentive to "hook it" in a new way. When a teacher's back was turned, a truant would bolt off. If this ruse was successful, a student was likely to hide out the next day and fail to appear for roll call.

Adolescents and children being what they are, adults assumed that nearly every student would skip school at least once. But even when performed as deftly as a fisherman's master stroke, the jerk of defiance doesn't always work. Parents and teachers know all the ropes—having learned them in their own days of playing hooky.

THROUGH THE GRAPEVINE

If you receive a message through the grapevine, it is likely to be gossip. That is because the new-fangled system of communication invented by Samuel F. B. Morse used wires that looked for all the world like vines strung between poles.

Especially during the Civil War, telegraph lines transmitted many wild rumors. Some of them spread so rapidly that soldiers and civilians alike agreed that there must be a "grapevine telegraph" at work in remote regions.

Most battlefield dispatches were true, but some were unfounded. Enough bogus or suspect messages were transmitted that any person-to-person network came to be labeled a *grapevine telegraph* whose news shouldn't be accepted without question.

THUNDERSTRUCK

As late as the seventeenth century, few common folk knew that thunder is the noise that follows a lightning flash. Many people caught outdoors in a violent storm feared thunderbolts almost as much as lightning.

Fear and trembling were so common during storms that these atmospheric disturbances were linked with any state of acute terror. A seventeenth-century poet described a love-shaken youth as being so "thunder-stroken" that he was "void of sense."

Since the time of Benjamin Franklin, we have known that thunder is never dangerous. But earlier notions about it are firmly embedded in language. As a result, a person who seems speechless from surprise or fear is likely to be described as being *thunderstruck*.

CHAPTER 11

JOKING AROUND

Everyday speech often includes barbed humor not always easily recognized. Human nature being what it is, those who first learned to babble in single-syllable words probably used some of them to poke fun at others. We use many inherited verbal jibes—and are constantly inventing new ones.

Cold-Blooded
Dark Horse
Fifth Wheel
Funny Bone
Henpeck
Know Beans
Left Holding the Bag
Lowbrow
Mug
Not Worth a Hill of Beans
Pull the Wool Over One's Eyes

COLD-BLOODED

Long before the rise of scientific medicine, everyday experience showed that there are strong links between emotions and blood. During anger or after activity, sensations in the face and neck hint that the vital fluid has become warmer. Feelings that accompany acute fear can be interpreted to mean that temperature of blood has suddenly dropped.

Medieval scholars found it striking that temperaments vary widely. Some people easily become enraged—so furious that their blood seems to be at the boiling point. Others seldom lose their tranquility, so may be derided as "passionless" or "cold-blooded."

Modern science has torpedoed the myth of wide variations in blood temperature among humans. But influence of the past and the association of cold-blooded reptiles with evil made a lasting impression upon speech.

Practically everyone now knows that a thermometer would show a healthy person's blood to be at 98.6 degrees or thereabouts. In spite of that, we still describe anyone considered cruel or vindictive as "being cold-blooded."

DARK HORSE

From the beginning of the democratic experiment, election of public officials has been seen as being a lot like a horse race. No one knows who will win until the votes are counted, but almost everyone has a favorite. So no disparagement is intended when a public figure compares a candidate with a spirited horse.

Legend has it that Sam Flynn of Tennessee picked up an easy living by racing a coal-black stallion named Dusky Pete. Flynn usually rode Pete into a strange town as though he were an ordinary saddle horse. Not knowing they faced a champion, local men cheerfully set up races—and lost. As a result, Flynn's dark horse became more than regionally noted.

Lingo of the track entered smoke-filled convention halls. As a result, professionals often joke that an unknown who shows a chance of winning is a "dark horse" in the campaign.

FIFTH WHEEL

Every so often you hear about an inventor who has come up with a way to create energy out of a new resource or process or element. Did you know there have been inventors who tried to turn water into gasoline? So far, no chemical or gadget has been successful with this idea.

Long before gasoline became a necessity of life, scammers took advantage of people always on the go. All sorts of contrivances were touted as adding efficiency or comfort to surreys and broughams and carriages.

One widely sold device was a horizontal wheel that attached to the front axle of a vehicle. On the rare occasion, this horizontal wheel provided a little support and stability during sharp turns. On good roads, however, this fifth wheel was a useless addition.

Except for the benefit of tourists, fifth wheels of this

sort—and vehicles that sport them—are long gone. Their influence was great enough, though, to form a teasing label for a person who is dateless in a group of partners.

FUNNY BONE

Human anatomy was largely a mystery until comparatively recent times. Because skeletons were abundant, bones were the first body parts to be the subject of scientific study. Terms to describe bones were chosen from Latin as it was the universal language of scholarship.

There is no record of who first gave serious attention to the relatively big bone that runs from the shoulder to the elbow, but it is technically known as the *humerus* (which is Latin for "upper arm").

Some jokester framed a pun and called the tip of the humerus "the funny bone." Bumping this bone is not humorous, even to those unacquainted with classical languages. Yet it yields a distinctively unusual—or funny—sensation when struck against a hard surface.

KNOW BEANS

More than a century ago, rural humor included a brief query: a person was asked to say how many blue beans it took to make seven white beans.

A person who gave up in bewilderment didn't know beans, of course, for the answer was simple: Seven blue beans, peeled, make seven white ones.

Anyone dull enough not to know beans may also be derided as "knowing diddly-squat."

LEFT HOLDING THE BAG

Rural America of the nineteenth century had no fraternities or sororities, but hazing was a common ritual. Often it involved taking an adolescent to hunt an imaginary bird, the snipe. Told that the snipe would dash into a heavy-duty bag that is properly held, the victim was made bag holder. Pranksters said they'd beat the bushes and drive the snipe into the bag—then slipped away, stifling their laughter.

When and where snipe hunting was invented, no one knows. But this rural method of poking fun at a gullible youngster was common. As a result, even in big cities where no one would wait for the imaginary snipe, a person who is tricked or swindled is said to be "left holding the bag."

LOWBROW

People who poke fun by calling someone a "lowbrow" usually think they are "highbrow." But they may not be aware that these labels perpetuate findings of a onetime science that has been completely discredited.

Seeking explanations for variations in intelligence, a group of nineteenth-century experimenters developed what they called *phrenology*, or the study of bumps and shapes of the skull.

Phrenologists swore that they could discern much from

a map of a person's head, with brows thought to be especially revealing. A person with high brows was judged to be especially intelligent, capable of doing almost anything. But anyone whose brows sat low on the forehead was supposedly a slob—doomed to ignorance from birth.

We now know that the height of a person's brow is meaningless except as a detail of appearance. Yet speech retains *lowbrow* to label anyone thought to lack refinement and incapable of acquiring it.

MUG

When you speak of a friend's face as his or her "mug," you make use of a relatively new word.

Beer mugs of the late eighteenth century were often shaped to represent human heads. Some depicted famous persons, others were caricatures of ordinary heads.

A person not especially noted for classical beauty often bore a more than superficial resemblance to a face on a mug. That inevitably led to joshing from friends and associates. As an aftermath of humor in the pottery shop, every face came to be called a *mug*.

NOT WORTH A HILL OF BEANS

Offered "a stand-out bargain" at a flea market, you may decline by silently or orally dismissing merchandise as being "not worth a hill of beans."

These days, you would be hard put to find a literal hill of

beans. But in the era when many households grew their own food, everyone had plenty of them.

A cluster of seeds covered with a mound of earth constituted a hill. Long rows in the garden included so many hills that no one bothered to count them. For practical purposes, this meant that a single hill of beans was so nearly worthless that its value couldn't be estimated.

PULL THE WOOL OVER ONE'S EYES

Only a few centuries ago, most men of importance wore large wigs. Since judges were especially dignified, they adopted appropriately prominent wigs.

Regardless of how skillful its maker, a woolen transformation for the head was likely to be clumsy. Many of them slipped in use, temporarily blocking vision.

A typical lawyer who succeeded in tricking a judge bragged and laughed simultaneously at having "pulled the wool over his eyes." Use in legal circles was so common that the expression came to stand for any ruse leading to deception.

CHAPTER 12

SOME THINGS ARE NOT
WHAT THEY SEEM

Compared with our language, clothing is almost childishly simple. A word or a phrase can have a contemporary connotation quite different from that of the past. Once you develop a pattern of looking beneath the surface of written and spoken words, you will discover that a few pages of a book or a few minutes of conversation will almost always involve usages that have undergone radical change.

Barge In
Bitter End
Black List
Double-Cross
Easy Street

BARGE IN

If you "barge into" a conference room and take a seat, your actions will not remotely resemble those of a clumsy cargo vessel. Yet movements of such a ship gave rise to our expression.

It was brought back to Europe by Crusaders who were impressed with a small sailing vessel they saw on the Nile river. Adapting the Egyptian name, similar ships built in Britain were called *barges*.

Especially designed for use in shallow water, the barge proved useful in canals as well as in rivers. Eventually steam replaced sails on these flat-bottom craft that were sturdy but clumsy. Accidents were frequent, for once a barge got under way it was difficult to stop it or to change course rapidly.

By 1800, shippers were comparing hasty action of any sort with the heavy rushing of a cargo boat. As a result, we continue to say that a person bursting into any situation is "barging into" it.

BITTER END

Many early English ships were equipped with a *bitt*, or heavy log mounted on an axle. With one end of a cable attached to the bitt, the other was tied to an anchor. Should anything happen to the bitt, a ship was in trouble—for there was no way to drop anchor in order to resist winds and tides.

In some waters, even a very long cable was not adequate. Played out until no more was wrapped around the bitt, the rope still didn't permit the anchor to touch bottom.

Such a situation was always alarming and often dangerous. As a result any unpleasant final result came to be called a "bitter end"—now often *bitter* is regarded as meaning an unpleasant taste in the mouth.

BLACK LIST

Deans of noted British colleges and universities often had to deal with misconduct. Many kept ledgers in which they recorded the names and misdeeds of students who broke rules. A dean's register of offenses was typically bound in black, so the records it held made up the "black list."

Owners of business firms were less precise about notebooks used in order to jot names of customers who didn't pay promptly. A record of people who should be denied credit took the campus label, in spite of the fact that a merchant's black list might be kept in a blue or brown book.

From these specialized usages, the "black list" expanded in meaning. Today it names any kind of records that identify those who should be denied membership or watched carefully.

DOUBLE-CROSS

In frontier America, a person unable to write was often required to sign a document. Under such circumstances, in lieu of a name it was legal to sign with an "X" on the form. Abraham Lincoln's mother followed this usage, along with multitudes of her contemporaries.

Often, a party to a contract agreed to it under pressure and didn't want to observe its terms. Oral lore insisted that when crosses were doubled, one being placed over the other, the first was cancelled or made null. Primitive as it sounds today, this double-cross was common enough to give its name to any act of deception or betrayal.

EASY STREET

Any time you find that a new acquaintance is living quite comfortably, you may think to yourself that they are living on "Easy Street."

This expression sounds as though it might have come from Bunyan, Dickens, or Thackeray. It is not difficult to picture a broad avenue bearing this name, perhaps located not far from London's famous Grub Street.

Oddly, though, the designation originated in the New World. It seems to have first appeared in print in a 1902 novel, which described a prosperous character as one who "could walk up and down Easy Street."

It seems logical to describe a person in comfortable

circumstances as having an address that summarizes their lifestyle. Catching the expression from the story titled "It's Up to You," *Easy Street* was soon widely familiar.

GRAVEYARD SHIFT

Every industry that operates around the clock has a *graveyard shift*. Some who punch a clock at odd hours think their time of work has some sort of connection with burial places. But the true origin is not quite so obvious.

Any thick liquid was called *gravy* for a long, long time. Only special kinds of gravy went on the table. "Humour running from the eyes" caused some people to be called "gravy-eyed."

In addition to disease, late vigils in bed led to bleary eyes. Sailors who had the watch that started at midnight were often gravy-eyed before they went off duty. That led them to speak of the middle watch as the "gravey-eyed shift."

Landlubbers who heard the expression didn't fully understand it. Aided by superstitions about cemeteries, the sea-born label became "the graveyard shift" in industry.

LOCK HORNS

When you comment that a pair of antagonists "lock horns," the expression may evoke an image of two angry steers going at one another head-to-head.

While such contests do take place in cattle pens, domestic animals did not give rise to the expression. It comes from the wilds of North America, where an old bull moose may boast antlers that weigh as much as sixty pounds.

Males are shy and unapproachable during most of the year, but become aggressive as the autumn mating season approaches. Nature affords few spectacles more dramatic than a pair of giant suitors with their spreading sets of horns locked in battle.

In frontier speech, angry humans were often compared with battling moose. As a result, we say that people who clash have "locked horns."

MARK TIME

When we say a person is forced to "mark time," we use an expression that seems to be based upon watching a clock. In its earliest usages, it had nothing to do with timepieces of any kind. Instead, the term stems from activities of drill sergeants about two hundred years ago, who demanded precision in movement.

One new exercise launched by the command "Mark time!" involved repeatedly lifting the feet without moving forward or backward. A soldier engaged in this drill expended a lot of energy, but got nowhere. As a result, the sergeant's command came to designate any futile activity by soldiers or civilians.

SECRETARY

A Latin term naming "a secret" gave rise to the English word *secretary*. People who held this title were originally in charge of the secret and confidential affairs of wealthy noblemen.

Many an early secretary soon discovered that correspondence required a great deal of time and energy. As writing letters became increasingly important, significance of the occupational title gradually shifted. Eventually any person employed to conduct correspondence—with or without secrets—took the old title.

Which means that present connotations of the label do not point to a secretary's earliest functions. Such titles as Secretary of State survive as a reminder that secretaries, now more widely known as "administrative assistants," are an invaluable asset to their organization—and you'd better treat them with respect, because they know the secrets.

SHOOT THE BULL

Confined in a pen, two or three bulls are likely to devote much of their energy to bellowing back and forth at one another. Experienced handlers know that the sounds produced, though frequent and loud, pose no threat. They are simply one way this male animal likes to make all in earshot aware of his presence.

Male humans, voluntarily penned in a room, tend to devote a lot of their energy to idle talk. Like noises made in a cattle pen, their sounds may mean very little—but seldom stop.

Inevitably, a fellow talking too much will be called down for his tendency to "shoot the bull," while a session in which several talk back and forth constitutes a "bull session."

CHAPTER 13

GOING PLACES

Though the automobile age has been very brief by comparison with eras of travel on foot and by use of animals, it has enriched language at interstate highway speed. Old or young, expressions created by our proclivity for going places may give no hint of their background until examined closely.

Automobile
Blowout
Coasting Along
Fast Lane
Holiday
Jeep
Pit Stop
Steering Wheel

AUTOMOBILE

Lots of those who got a look at early self-propelled vehicles laughed. "Better stick with the horse," they shouted.

H. H. Kohlsaat, owner of the *Chicago Times-Herald*, paid no attention. As a publicity stunt, he planned a race between contraptions that didn't use harnesses or reins. To sweeten the pot, he offered $500 for the best name for horseless wagons.

Inventors had already come up with "buggyaut," "auto-kinet," and "buckmobile." Three who entered the contest suggested "motorcycle," so prize money was split between these winners. "From now on," said the rich man from the Windy City, "*motorcycle* will name 'any kind of wagon driven by a steam plant, storage batteries, or a self-contained motor.'"

Hardly anybody paid any attention. Borrowing the Greek word *auto* for "self," and the French *mobile* for "moving," consumers began to call the self-moving wagon the *automobile*.

By 1910, the brand-new name (that didn't win a prize) was in general use among Americans, who spread it around the world.

BLOWOUT

Town and city folk picked up this expression coined by tellers of tall tales and used it to mean an outburst of anger.

By the time Washington Irving and Sir Walter Scott put it into their novels, everybody knew what "having a blowout" meant.

Davy Crockett is said to have used this phrase to describe a fellow who turned red in the face and started hollering.

But a rush of hot air from an early pneumatic tire made a blowout by a riverboat gambler seem tame. Seventy pounds of pressure against thin rubber on unpaved roads made tires almost as explosive as liquid refreshments at a big shindig.

Thicker, tougher tires and asphalt roads cut down on highway blowouts, so our living language turned back upon itself. With frontier emphases revived, you are now a lot more likely to be involved in a blowout in someone's living room or den than on the interstate.

COASTING ALONG

Captains of ocean-going vessels, facing weeks on the water, were early advocates of speed. A windjammer headed across the Atlantic was likely to have all sails spread when the wind was strong.

By contrast with fast ships of this sort, schooners that were involved in the coastal trade seemed to be slow, even leisurely. They traveled short distances, so their masters seldom bothered to use every possible yard of canvas.

Some vessels in coastal waters may have been more hurried than they seemed. Whether that was the case or not, their apparently casual movement became proverbial. As a result, a person far from water who shows no signs of effort or haste is still described as "coasting along."

FAST LANE
Until the automobile changed the nature and pace of society, no one talked about life in the "fast lane."

Builders of the New Jersey Turnpike, two lanes wide in both directions, had a revolutionary idea from the start. Traffic would flow much more freely, they suggested, if slow-moving vehicles were required to stay in the right lane.

Experiments showed that the concept was correct, and it soon became standard practice for fast-moving vehicles—initially cars only—to use the left lane. Highway practices spawned talk about "life in the fast lane," dangerous for everyone if adopted by slowpokes behind the wheel or anywhere else.

HOLIDAY
In medieval England, a "holy day" was designed primarily for worship, and no ordinary tasks were performed. Enforced leisure made it inevitable that festivals and amusements should begin to flourish at such a time. Now marked by fun and worship, old verbal elements combined and the period of observance came to be known as a *holiday*.

Some religious groups still emphasize a holy day at intervals, and many nations observe legal holidays on which official business is not conducted.

Holdovers from the past remain influential. Yet the holiday notion is now strongly linked with taking a trip. Those for whom a holy day once meant freedom from work in order to worship would be hard put to comprehend the modern holiday on wheels or in the air.

JEEP

Elzie Crisler Segar is far from a household name. But comic strip characters he created are known everywhere. Popeye the Sailor, launched circa 1930, made a quick and lasting hit.

Eugene the Jeep, an animal friend of Popeye, appeared on March 16, 1936. Slender but very strong, he was widely admired by readers.

Soon after becoming acquainted with Eugene the Jeep, soldiers began working with a new vehicle. Small and drab, the sturdy car had four drive wheels instead of the then-standard two.

Military supply officers initially stenciled the little heavy-duty car *GP*—for "general purpose." Influenced by its initials, GIs compared the new vehicle with Eugene the Jeep. As a result, both the military Jeep and its civilian relatives perpetuate the name of a remarkable animal made famous by a comic strip.

PIT STOP

The advent of the automobile created a need for a special kind of pit, or hole in the ground. Heavy-duty hydraulic jacks with which to lift cars had not come into vogue. In order to make repairs or add grease to the suspension, a mechanic could wriggle about on his back—or crawl into a pit.

At the Indianapolis raceway, the place where mechanics worked had little in common with the customer service station except for the familiar name stuck to it. To a driver needing fuel or new tires, a pit stop was essential even though it meant the loss of precious seconds.

Importance of the pit stop at the Indy 500 and later races added color and variety to everyday speech. As a result, an interstate highway traveler in desperate need of a restroom or a cup of coffee is likely to make a "pit stop" at a place which has no pit.

STEERING WHEEL

Henry Ford's hand-built car of 1896 wasn't easily guided. Any sailor could see that its cumbersome steering device, or *tiller*, was modeled after those used on ships.

For his "No. 999" car, the first racing car driven by Barney Oldfield, Ford scrapped the tiller in favor of a cranking device. It proved so clumsy that in 1903 he offered steering by means of a wheel.

Rival makers adopted the steering wheel about the same time as Ford. Prospective buyers to whom it was shown were assured that abandonment of the tiller severed all ties between ships and autos.

So they thought! Many veteran drivers remembered that

steering wheels were used on ships as early as 1750. An engineering manual described such a device as the "wheel that guides a ship, giving motion to the rudder by means of a tiller rope."

Which means that anyone behind the steering wheel during rush-hour traffic may still find themselves "at sea" after all.

STEP ON IT

Engineering changes enabled motorists to pick up speed rapidly before World War I. Some models still used hand throttles to regulate the flow of fuel, but most employed the relatively new "foot feed" not yet commonly called the *accelerator*.

Known by whatever name, the foot-controlled mechanism freed both hands for steering. That meant a driver could keep a car on the road even when moving from ten to forty miles per hour in seconds. Reporting such an exploit, a driver was likely to talk about having "stepped on the gas."

Regardless of whether or not you drive a car with a foot feed, when planning to speed up action of any sort, it is customary to announce intentions to "step on it."

TWO-WAY STREET

Introduction of automobiles created a demand for new and better rural roads. At the same time, the new vehicles posed fresh problems in many cities—especially those of Europe. A cobblestone boulevard wide enough to permit vehicles to pass one another and hence to move in either direction is still a rarity in a few larger cities like Lisbon, Madrid, and Paris.

In land-rich America, wide streets are commonplace. Since traffic moves simultaneously in both directions on such a thoroughfare, we speak of any situation or relationship that can be approached from opposite directions as a "two-way street."

CHAPTER 14

FOOD LANGUAGE

Not only is one person's food another's poison, the language of food in one era may be something altogether different in succeeding ones. Some expressions that seem to point directly to food have little or nothing to do with the table. Others that are deeply rooted in food have taken on new meanings so distinct and familiar that association with eating can be seen only dimly and after careful scrutiny.

Adam's Apple
Groggy
Half-Baked
Hot Dog
Hot Potato
Humble Pie
No Bones
Potluck

Rehash
Sandwich

ADAM'S APPLE

Many a man, such as Abraham Lincoln, has had a prominent Adam's apple. Male chauvinism is responsible for the
centuries-old name.

Pioneer English anatomists were puzzled by the section of cartilage that refused to stay in one spot. Folktales
explained that Adam should not have taken that apple from
Eve in the Garden of Eden. When he yielded to her temp-
tation, a piece of fruit stuck on the way down. Ever since, it
has moved when men eat or talk in order to warn; "Beware
of the temptress!"

In truth, the growth of the visible knot is stimulated by
male hormones. Because women have a small amount of this
hormone, they also have a small version of the Adam's apple.

GROGGY

Any time you get up in the morning feeling a bit groggy, take
pity on eighteenth-century British sailors.

Admiral Edward Vernon was a fine-looking figure standing on the poop deck of a vessel wearing a luxurious coat.
Many of the men under his command despised him and as a
gesture of contempt, they used "Old Grog" to name the man
identified by his grogram coat.

At the height of his career, the admiral issued an order

that was brand-new to Her Majesty's navy. Henceforth and hereafter, he stipulated, every cask of rum must be diluted with water before any drinks were served. Furious sailors gave the watered-down beverage the name *grog*, after the man who had invented it.

Even though it wasn't as potent as rum, grog could make a fellow dizzy in short order. Hence, anyone inclined to wobble while walking came to be described as being *groggy*.

HALF-BAKED

Each type of bread and pastry not only has its special recipe of ingredients—it also must be baked at the proper temperature and for the right length of time.

A person learning to bake is often afraid of burning their product. As a result, a beginner is likely to take bread out of the oven too soon. Once cooled and cut, it cannot be put back for additional baking.

Anyone or anything raw or incomplete or foolish is likely to be called *half-baked*—about as desirable as under-cooked products of the oven.

HOT DOG

No one knows who was first to put links of mild sausage into long buns and serve them hot. Requiring no implements in order to be eaten, the new delicacy proved a hit when vendors began selling it on the streets of cities.

At first, the German word for this special food was *frankfurter,* and later its kin *wienerwurst* appeared. Both were soon clipped to *franks* and *wieners.*

But the abbreviated labels seemed tame and non-descriptive. Vendors and devotees decided that the long and lean sausage resembled the body of a prized pet. That is why the slender and low-slung dachshund inspired the wiener-wurst in a soft bun to take the name that is now universal: *hot dog.*

HOT POTATO

A hardy plant that yielded big red tubers was discovered by early explorers of North America. It was taken to England quite early, but attracted little attention except among botanists. Regarded as a curiosity, it had only one known use: when dried and powdered, a tuber provided an abundant supply of what was thought to be an aphrodisiac.

While English gentry dropped powder into their drinks, American farmers began experimenting with the plant. They found the tuber to be wholesome and appetizing and began to call it a *sweet potato.*

As the sweet potato was easily baked, it gradually became a staple of farm life. Impatient boys and girls seemed never to learn that a potato hot from the ashes must be left to cool.

Erupting from speech of rural households, *hot potato* came to stand for any problem too hot to handle.

HUMBLE PIE

Although we do not use the expression as frequently as our ancestors did, it is not uncommon to hear someone refer to eating "humble pie."

For centuries, dainty pies were made of the *umbles*, or intestines, of sheep. Just as chitterlings from intestines of swine are regarded as delicacies in many quarters today, umble pie was considered a mouthwatering confection in medieval England.

Differences in pronunciation led people to add an initial letter that transformed the meaning of the ancient term. Seldom available from the kitchen of a manor house these days, *humble pie* has come to be linked with humiliation rather than feasting.

NO BONES

Especially when made with fish, stew or soup is likely to include a few bones. Large fragments seldom cause trouble, but tiny slivers may bring discomfort or worse.

When a cook points to the pot and assures family members or guests that "there are no bones," that is a signal to dig in. No need to pause in order to check for the presence of a tooth-jarring or gum-pricking bone.

Sometimes a person who speaks with no hesitation conjures up a vision of someone eating a boneless stew. They don't pause; they go right for it. Especially when frankness is deliberate and premeditated, the speaker is said to make "no bones" about telling it exactly as it is.

POTLUCK

Medieval gentry usually had plenty of rich food, frequently serving four or five kinds of meat at a meal. But families in the lower economic classes had no such abundance. Often a struggle was required to get enough food to prevent hunger.

In order to stretch her food, the wife of a commoner would keep an iron pot on an open fire. She threw all her leftovers into it each day, and kept it simmering much of the time. If a relative arrived unexpectedly, he was likely to have to eat from the pot without having any idea of what odds and ends had gone into it.

This early and literal form of taking "potluck" came to name the act of eating any meal for which the host or hostess has made no special preparation.

REHASH

English squires, long famous for their hearty appetites, were depicted with ridicule in the classic novel *Tom Jones* by Henry Fielding. Many of these folks wasted as much meat as they ate, but artisans and craftsmen and others tried never to throw away food.

At a middle-class inn where guests expected meat on the table, the landlord couldn't afford to toss away a shoulder after the choice slices were cut from it. So cooks often made hash from leftovers and guests usually complained. If they pushed hash aside, they were likely to get it the following day in the form of meat loaf.

Such a warmed-over dish, scornfully dubbed a *rehash,* was served frequently. So many persons ate it, willingly or reluctantly, that we've expanded the meaning of its name. Now we use it not just to label leftover food, but to designate a debate or speech in which old arguments are trotted out, thinly disguised by new words.

SANDWICH

Anytime you eat a sandwich, you help to perpetuate the memory of an English nobleman in the eighteenth century.

John Montagu, fourth Earl of Sandwich, became first lord of the admiralty in 1748. Any time he could slip away from his offices for an hour or two, he indulged his passion for gambling. Since his time was usually limited, he often directed a servant to bring him roast beef between slices of bread so he could eat at the gambling table.

He may not have been the first to enjoy this concoction, but he was clearly the only world leader who did so frequently in public. As a result, his royal title attached to this early form of fast food, and *sandwich* soon became familiar throughout the world.

CHAPTER 15

BORROWED FROM BRITISH

For centuries the United Kingdom was the primary developer of the English language. Some of their distinctive expressions have not been adopted, but many have become popular in the United States. Though Americans have picked up phrases from all shores, those coming from the island kingdom have been the most abundant.

Bonfire
Fork Over
Gadget
Keep a Stiff Upper Lip
Masterpiece
On the House
Poll
Rigmarole
Sidekick

BONFIRE

There is nothing quite like the combination of festivity and food at an evening picnic that includes a bonfire.

This source of fun and frolic is particularly American, but we borrowed the word *bonfire* from our English ancestors. It once referred to a *bone-fire*, which was a primitive form of cremation. After the practice was abandoned by ordinary folk, it was observed with bodies of saints. Ashes from the burning of a saint's bones were potent good luck charms.

When roaring blazes ceased to be used to consume bones, the spelling of *bone-fire* changed, and any hearty outdoor fire came to be known as a *bonfire*.

FORK OVER

Noblemen owned most of Britain's good farmland until modern times. Peasants who wanted to rent were required to promise to pay in silver.

At harvest time, landlords sent collection agents for the annual rent—often before crops could be sold. A tenant without silver had to make payment in kind with his produce.

Shrewd agents often allowed less than market value for grain or other staples accepted in lieu of silver. So a farmer forced to deliver his rent with a pitchfork cursed under his breath while making his payment.

GADGET

No kitchen or toolshed is complete without assorted gizmos that look impressive but aren't very useful. When you need help in reaching one of them and cannot remember what to call it, you are likely to request: "Please hand me that gadget from the shelf."

Sailors in Britain's vast merchant marine gave us this indispensable term, which they adapted from French. Impressed with small mechanical parts of new-style rifles made across the English Channel, nineteenth-century seamen stumbled over the French word *gâchette*. Already used in France to label any small mechanism—from guns to locks— the English sailors adopted *gadget* for the same purpose.

Responding to what they claim is consumer demand, manufacturers now load cars, stereos, and other devices with conspicuous gadgets that may be more costly than helpful. As every aficionado knows, any widget or dingus of this sort is at least distantly related to some earlier gadget.

KEEP A STIFF UPPER LIP

For at least a dozen centuries, men of England alternated between shaving and growing whiskers. Razors were used every day during most of the reign of Queen Anne. To make up for what the razor took, many a sporting fellow donned a wig. When wigs were abandoned by most people except barristers, facial hair made a comeback.

Soldiers may have been first to give up beards in favor of

mustaches. But military men who grew them discovered a serious drawback. Hair on the upper lip, no matter how carefully clipped and waxed, moves at the slightest twitch of a muscle.

Many a seasoned officer, himself slow to adopt the newfangled mustache, shouted and commanded orders. If a young fellow insisted upon growing hair under his nose, he would have to learn to keep a stiff upper lip. Movements of a mustache when standing rigidly at attention might even be considered a breach of discipline.

Spreading from barracks-room talk of men hoping to become known as officers and gentlemen, the phrase came to label self-control in any difficult situation.

MASTERPIECE

Trade guilds of past eras required an apprentice to learn by working under a veteran for nearly nothing, perhaps for years. The guilds stipulated that a person wishing to own their own shop had to be recognized as a *master*. After working for years as an apprentice, and later as a journeyman, a man could make a piece in his craft that would be considered that of a master's.

Once a man's "master piece" was approved, he was allowed to start his own business and hire an apprentice. For the rest of his life, he might look back upon his master piece as the finest example of his skill and ingenuity.

Passing from trade and industry of England to the fine arts, the term *masterpiece* came to label the finest individual piece of work or any product of an artist's most creative years.

ON THE HOUSE

Anything distributed free of charge, courtesy of the management, is "on the house."

Originally, the house involved was an English pub or tavern. Owners often invited newcomers to sample their stock by offering a free drink. This small taste often whetted the appetite for more, and the barkeep could expect the sale of several more drinks.

Some US states prohibit a barkeeper from offering freebies; in other regions, rising costs have made the custom obsolete. Despite this, we say that gifts to a consumer from a business owner are "on the house."

POLL

Hardly a week goes by without the announcement of results from a poll—newspapers, social media, online quizzes, politics, etc. Techniques that users consider to be scientific have made poll results newsworthy, regardless of the topic.

Polling activities, which sometimes seriously impact public opinion, are rooted in practices from Britain's historic past. In the United Kingdom, there were early census-takers, but they didn't ask a series of questions. They simply counted heads in order to learn how many people lived in a town or borough. The word *poll* is of Germanic origin, and first occurs in English in the thirteenth century, when it meant "a head." Therefore, counting heads meant "counting polls."

So even today when results are not physically conducted,

but tallied by computer software, in its literal sense a *poll* is simply a count of heads.

RIGMAROLE

Although origin of the title is obscure, *ragman* was the designation applied to a feudal official by a statute instituted by Edward I of England. When he invaded Scotland in 1296, his aides forced all nobles and gentry to sign a ragman's roll as a token of allegiance. Once they finally complied, the king sent couriers all over the country reading these lists. He hoped that announcing the submission of leaders would bring resistance of the ordinary folk to an end.

Whether from weariness or carelessness, Edward's messengers reeled off the names so quickly that they were difficult to understand. Hence any jumble of words was compared with a flow of names and called a *ragman's roll.*

Streamlined from frequent use, the old term for the loyalty list, now *rigmarole*, changed to mean a nearly incoherent jumble of fast-flowing words. Over time *rigmarole* has expanded its meaning and also refers to a long and complicated process that is annoying and seems unnecessary.

SIDEKICK

Pickpockets abounded in London and other English cities during the time of Victorian author Charles Dickens. These pickpockets were organized in tight-knit groups much like modern youth gangs. A recruit had to go through an apprenticeship, much as though he were in training for an honorable craft.

Pickpockets developed their own slang vocabulary. In their speech a *pratt* was a hip pocket, while a *pit* was a breast pocket. They used *jerve* to name a vest pocket and *kick* to designate a side pocket in a pair of breeches.

Even a veteran of this special kind of crime was likely to have trouble with a kick. It lay close to a potential victim's leg, and was in constant motion. Street-smart London merchants learned that money placed there was safer than that in any other pocket.

It became proverbial that a fellow who didn't want to lose his bundle should stash it in his "sidekick." As a result, any faithful partner always at one's side took the name of the trousers pocket that is most resistant to pickpockets.

SKELETONS IN THE CLOSET

English physicians eager to learn more about the human body were long under severe restrictions. Only the body of an executed criminal could be dissected until a controversial Anatomy Act was passed in 1832.

Many an early doctor dissected only one cadaver during his career. Naturally, he prized the skeleton highly and didn't want to dispose of it. Yet public opinion warned against keeping it where it might be seen. So the prudent anatomist hung his prize in a dark corner where visitors were not likely to discover it.

Patients weren't complete numbskulls, however. Most knew or suspected that their physician had a skeleton in his closet. From this literal sense, the phrase expanded to indicate hidden evidence of any kind.

WITCH'S BREW

Neither witches nor their male counterparts, warlocks, commonly pretended to be in league with the devil. Most were herbalists and midwives, while others charged fees for peering into the future or the secrets of nature.

Popular thought credited a witch with supernatural power even if she didn't claim it. To ordinary folk, such a woman seemed to be forever boiling some mysterious brew in a cauldron—often a homemade cold remedy. When ready for use, this potent stuff was believed capable of influencing the fate of individuals and nations. Shakespeare immortalized the concept when in Macbeth he described "dreadful charms" simmering in a big iron pot.

Despite modern health concerns and the growing desire for natural ingredients, few today bend over pots in order to concoct a witch's brew. But the name of the mysterious stuff lives on in speech to designate any potent compound prepared with unknown motives.

CHAPTER 16

STORIES TO BE TAKEN
WITH A GRAIN OF SALT

Sleuths seeking the origins of words, better known as *etymologists*, often confess failure. Evidence may be lacking or confused, causing scholars to note that there is no plausible explanation for the particular usage of a word or a phrase.

Since nature abhors a vacuum, imagination often rushes in where scholarship fails. Numerous accounts of the way an expression was formed are products of folk etymology. That is, ordinary folk make up explanations that are transmitted orally before breaking into print. Because of their intrinsic interest, such accounts are not to be dismissed out of hand.

Rather, they are to be savored for what they are—verbal flights on wings of ostriches.

Booze
Charley Horse
Crocodile Tears
Elbow Room
Hogwash
Knock on Wood
Monkey Wrench
On the Nose
Pull Up Stakes
See Red

BOOZE

Little to nothing is known about Philadelphia merchant E. G. Booze, says tradition, except that he is commemorated in everyday speech. According to a common story, he bought moonshine whiskey anywhere he could get it. Then he resold the whiskey. A bottle shaped like a log cabin was his standard container, but it lacked the customary maker's label.

Customers who liked Booze's prices didn't quibble over brand names, and applied his name, rather than the original merchant's name, to his bottle. Since Philadelphia was a major city, its term for unlabeled whiskey spread from that center into every town and village.

That story about E. G. Booze seems to have taken shape because there is no solid evidence about the origin of the word that is now universally familiar.

Another possibility is rooted in an old Dutch term *búsen* meaning "to drink to excess," but that word disappeared from use for generations. Revived perhaps four centuries ago, *búsen* began to be spelled as it sounds, producing the universally familiar but mystery-shrouded *booze*.

CHARLEY HORSE

Many a gym goer or athletic trainer could probably share why you call a muscular spasm a *charley horse*. However, their stories are sure to differ.

One story is that at the old Chicago White Sox ballpark, there was an old horse named Charley. All during the 1890s, he was used to pull a roller across the infield. His work was repetitive, so his leg muscles got so stiff he could hardly walk. Players and spectators who suddenly caught a cramp thought of the old fellow, and called it a *charley horse*.

Though that explanation doesn't hold up under scrutiny, it survives because there is no solid alternative. Before veterinary science was widely known, jockeys and trainers used *horse ail* to name any obscure ailment of a racer. In the same era, a night watchman was a *charlie*—whose pounding of the cobblestones probably produced many an aching muscle. Foot or leg cramps experienced by a charlie could have been compared with ailments of a lame animal in order to produce the term *charley horse.* Both are more probable than the Chicago-based story of the ballpark horse.

CROCODILE TEARS

Greek and Roman explorers who first encountered the awesome crocodile came home with a bundle of tall tales. According to them, the creature with a huge mouthful of teeth moaned like a woman in distress in order to lure victims within snapping distance.

Once a person went down the crocodile's path, the animal sobbed out of pity for its most recent meal. At least, that was the story circulated centuries ago and used by writers as late as the time of Shakespeare.

The tall tale was repeated orally for generation after generation. As a result, stories about "crocodile tears" caused any bogus show of contrition to take that name.

ELBOW ROOM

Many British soldiers and Hessian mercenaries who fought under General John Burgoyne had one thing in common: they despised the aristocratic commander whose peers knew him as "Gentleman Johnny."

According to a story dating from the American Revolution, Burgoyne was much better at bragging than at fighting. Arriving in the vast region he was sent to subdue, he boasted that he would have plenty of elbowroom in which to operate.

His remark, says legend, caused *elbowroom* to become a label for a maximum of space. That makes a story good enough to appear in more than one reputable source. But it is hard to believe that a single casual remark could have lasting impact.

What could be more natural than to say that an area adequate for work or leisure gives a person room to move the elbows? As a term for a minimum of space, elbowroom was in use two centuries before Burgoyne's birth. That makes it highly improbable that Gentleman Johnny had anything to do with the fact that we continue to use this expression today.

HOGWASH

In Old England, male swine were often castrated so that their meat would remain tender and juicy. The castrated males were called *hogs*. This practice was followed by a ceremonial washing, after which the water was thrown out as worthless. This, according to oral tradition, gave rise to the expression *hogwash*.

That makes a good story, but the real origin of *hogwash* involved neither castration nor cleansing. For generations this was the common name of swill fed to swine. Since the watery stuff might include no nourishment except table scraps and a little flour, it hardly rated as genuine food.

Exaggerated claims and tall tales are "verbal hogwash," or talk that is not substantial.

KNOCK ON WOOD

It is common practice to "knock on wood" with knuckles in order to try to ward off trouble or to seek good fortune. Almost invariably, this action is accompanied by a verbal announcement that it is taking place.

Ask a dozen acquaintances how this started, and at least one is likely to say that knocking turns a person's thoughts to the wooden cross on which Christ was crucified.

Knocking on wood as a form of asking for luck may just as easily stem from the play of children.

In many forms of the game of tag, trees afford sanctuary. A child who tags an oak or a pine is momentarily free from capture. But such knocking on wood doesn't count unless it is accompanied by a shout of triumph. That is, both actions and an announcement are required in order to assure the good luck that comes from safety.

MONKEY WRENCH

A friend or associate doesn't have to sport a long tail in order to throw a *monkey wrench* into plans and disrupt them.

One report has it that London craftsman Charles Moncke invented this special form of wrench and gave it his name. But even today, the British say "adjustable spanner" and not "monkey wrench." Another account would have you believe that the monkey wrench was developed by an American named Monk. No one has ever been able to find evidence that the tool was named for the first person to make it. A more probable explanation is that the people who first saw it may have laughed heartily. After all, a wrench whose lower jaw goes down or up at a twist of the fingers is about as ludicrous as a monkey jawing at onlookers in a zoo.

ON THE NOSE

Some folks will tell you that *on the nose,* meaning "exactly right," comes from the racetrack. While it may seem logical, the phrase comes from the studio, not the track.

Directors of early radio programs found that they often had to communicate with people in front of live microphones. In order to give directions without making sounds, a special sign language was developed. When a program was running precisely on schedule, the person watching the time put a finger alongside his or her nose.

So a horse who wins "by a nose" has nothing to do with this familiar expression, which finally appeared in print in the 1930s.

PULL UP STAKES

A person restless at work and not happy with the climate or job opportunities may be ready to *pull up stakes* and go elsewhere.

This expression, from a commonly told tale, owes its existence to Phineas T. Barnum's great American circus. Seldom spending more than two or three nights in one location, the circus was performed in tents, with ropes secured by stakes driven into the ground. When the circus moved, pulling up the stakes came to be synonymous with moving.

Though it sounds great, that explanation is a long way off the target. When public land in the West was grabbed by a homesteader, they were expected to stay within survey lines marked by stakes. But many a greedy fellow went out after dark, pulled up the stakes and relocated them to suit himself.

Legality of such action was rarely challenged. Today, a person who wouldn't know a boundary marker if he met it in the middle of the street is said to "pull up stakes" when an old location is abandoned in favor of a new one.

SEE RED

If you "see red" once in a while, you're normal—occasional anger is an ingredient in the mix we call living. But do not rebuke yourself for a brief incident that makes you seem like a bull who is being taunted by matadors.

That was the story circulated to explain why a show of temper is linked with red rather than with, say, purple or yellow. Tradition says that red banners or clothing are used by bullfighters in order to infuriate animals.

There is no truth to the story, though it has circulated for many years. Scientific tests have shown that bulls pay no more attention to red than to other colors. It is the waving of fabric or movement of a matador that catches an animal's eye and induces him to charge.

At least one investigator says that the waving of a white

cloth will enrage a bull even more quickly than movements of a red cloth. Even if that is gospel truth, it won't affect our everyday speech. For generations to come, our descendants will still be saying that a person who indulges in a visible burst of temper is seeing red.

CHAPTER 17

COMPARISONS THAT
FROZE IN SPEECH

Any activity or event that attracts enough interest and attention can cause someone to make comparisons. Once a new term fashioned in this way becomes widely used, it may remain vital for decades or for centuries. In many instances, a word or a phrase does not immediately reveal the comparison that brought it into being.

Assembly Line
Big Shot
Bulldozer
Chime In
Dead as a Doornail
Fishy
Fit as a Fiddle

Jumping-Off Place
Straitlaced
Taper Off

ASSEMBLY LINE

At first, cars weren't mass-produced; they were made by hand one at a time. Henry Ford got the idea of mass-producing his cars from watching an overhead trolley in a Chicago packing plant. In order to build automobiles in large quantities Ford had Model T flywheel magnetos move slowly past workers in a line, who performed only one or two building operations each.

Production soared four hundred percent, so he moved from mass-producing magnetos, to engines and transmissions, and then to complete cars. Model Ts in the making, conveyed at six feet per minute past workers who used standardized parts, were sold at prices not imagined when cars were handmade luxuries. Ford launched modern mass production, yet the workers soon complained that their jobs were monotonous.

Even when performed at the keyboard of a computer instead of beside a conveyor belt, any highly repetitive work is likely to be criticized as "an assembly line job."

BIG SHOT

Largely self-taught, John A. B. Dahlgren designed some of the largest guns used in the Civil War. A cannon that took his name, immense at the breech and tapering toward the muzzle, played decisive roles in numerous battles.

A sailor or soldier who saw an eleven-inch Dahlgren for the first time was often speechless. This big gun made earlier ones seem tiny and powerless. Fighting men compared an admiral or a general with the huge weapon and called the man in command a *big gun*.

Since Dahlgren's big guns spewed big shot at the enemy, any person of great importance was also known as a *big shot*.

BULLDOZER

In the aftermath of the Civil War, many Louisiana former overseers called themselves *bulldozers*. The punishment overseers had traditionally exacted upon enslaved people was, inhumanely, likened to doses of punishment fit for a bull and also possibly due to the fact that many overseers carried a bullwhip used to intimidate by violence.

Long dormant, this negatively charged name was revived prior to World War II. It seemed an appropriate word to designate a powerful earth-moving machine that easily pushed opposition aside.

After being widely used in military operations, the mechanical bulldozer became standard equipment in construction work.

CHIME IN

Well before the fourteenth century, an unknown musician discovered that bells can be rung by striking them. Music produced in such fashion came to be known as *chimes*, usually involving a simple melody repeated many times. After the first chord is struck, other bells simply echo it.

Conversations often resemble the chimes from a cathedral tower. A person of importance will give an opinion, and those who hear it will mumble agreement.

Resemblance between harmony from a bell tower and speech by anyone who echoes another's opinion causes us to say that such a person does little except "chime in."

DEAD AS A DOORNAIL

Anything from a withered houseplant to a failed project that is beyond resurrection is likely to be described as being "dead as a doornail."

Both mechanical and electric doorbells are recent inventions. In earlier centuries, a visitor's arrival was announced by pounding with a knocker upon a metal plate nailed to the door.

Sometimes it took several heavy blows to attract attention. That meant nails holding the knocking plate suffered a lot of punishment. Repeatedly hit on its head, such a nail had the life pounded out of it so effectively that nothing could be deader.

FISHY

Benjamin Disraeli, first earl of Beaconsfield, is famous as having been a prime minister of England, making his way up the political ladder against great opposition. Had it not been for his brilliant wit and colorful use of language, he might have remained a small-time politician.

Disraeli wrote the novel *Coningsby* in order to influence public opinion. As he had done in earlier novels, the statesman tried to write as people talk and made many comparisons. As a result of this style, a famous piece of description includes a comment about the "most fishy thing I ever saw." The odor of fish made him think of dubious political deals, Disraeli observed, noting also that both fish and politicians may be slippery.

Brought into speech by the writer-statesman, the new expression came into general use to label any situation that includes suspicious elements.

FIT AS A FIDDLE

In one form or another, the stringed fiddle was popular in England nearly a thousand years ago. Sizes and shapes varied, as did the number and length of strings.

All early fiddles were handmade, and most were used in rural settings. Listeners as well as players knew when the tension of the strings was not right or when an instrument was warped. Only an undamaged fiddle that was properly adjusted was in top shape, or "fit" to use with an audience.

Hundreds of years later, a person in vigorous good health is still said to be as "fit as a fiddle"—undamaged and well-tuned, that is.

JUMPING-OFF PLACE

During the era in which the frontier was flowing westward, trading posts represented civilization's last fringe. Traders who ran their prices sky-high were likely to have only a few criminals and adventurers as neighbors.

Many people preferred open country to spots infested with two-legged skunks. But a fellow planning to jump into the wilderness had to go to a trading post for supplies. Almost every spoken and written reference to such a "jumping-off place" was disparaging. Adopted by those who had never been outside a city, the frontier term is now used to label any remote area or the spot for beginning a journey.

STRAITLACED

Should someone describe you as "straitlaced," your views will determine whether to regard this as complimentary or disparaging. For the old garment term may be interpreted either way.

Elaborate corsets were sometimes worn in classical times. But the garment didn't become widely popular until a few centuries ago. In the gilded era that followed discovery of the New World, new garments came into fashion, especially for ladies of great wealth. For the sake of fashion, a grand dame might pull her bodice so tight that her waist seemed to shrink. Since anything tight and narrow was called *strait*, a woman strapped into a whale-bone corset was literally "laced strait," or *straitlaced*.

It was inevitable that comparisons should be made. As early as 1526 a person of strict convictions was given the name of a woman laced into a corset so tightly that she could hardly breathe.

TAPER OFF

Fire has been associated with worship since prehistoric times, a practice that led to use of candles, or *tapers*, as symbols of purity and devotion.

Early candles were crude, but worshippers gradually learned how to make long, graceful ones that would burn for hours. Beeswax was and still is employed for many of the finest. Hand-dipped, such a taper is distinctive in shape. Gradually growing smaller, it comes to a definite point at the top.

From the shape of a fine candle, a colorful comparison entered general speech. Anything that diminishes gradually, whether it gives off light or not, is said to "taper off."

CHAPTER 18

ACTION IS THE NAME
OF THE GAME

Many of our familiar expressions are based upon actions of the past, and action of one sort or another is indicated by many words and phrases that appear to be static. Here's hoping your happiness index will rise as you become more familiar with terms of action.

Backseat Driver
Bandwagon
Blow Off Steam
Fly Off the Handle
Hocus Pocus
Live Wire

Pull the Plug
Railroad
Siren
Whistleblower

BACKSEAT DRIVER

Barney Oldfield's Ford No. 999 held only the driver. Single seats of some early cars held two or three people. Rear seats weren't added until the auto age was beyond its infancy. A backseat held additional riders, but those riding in the back found it difficult to talk to the driver.

In 1912, things began to change. The four-cylinder Essex coach was offered with a box-like body that was comfortably enclosed. Other makers soon copied the idea.

Passengers immediately took advantage of their chance to be heard. Calling for action or telling the person at the wheel where to turn or stop, the backseat driver caused this name to label any person who volunteers advice to the one in charge.

BANDWAGON

America's first great showman, Phineas T. Barnum, didn't wait for the public to come to him. Instead, he took his attractions to the people. Arriving in a city for an engagement, he would hire a high wagon of the sort used by local bands of musicians for outdoor performances.

Parading through streets with odd-looking men and women aboard wagons, "Barnum's Great Scientific and Musical Theater" was a sensation. Onlookers were encouraged to hop on the bandwagons in order to ride with the performers and add to the excitement.

Many political clubs built bandwagons of their own, then gave rolling concerts to publicize candidates. The impact of Barnum and elections on speech proved lasting. Any person who agrees to become a part of a movement, campaign, or simply joins the crowd is described as "climbing on the bandwagon."

BLOW OFF STEAM

It took years for trainmen to learn how to handle locomotives. Hot fires were required in order to keep up enough steam to move. But when an engine halted, steam pressure could rise quickly. There were no safety valves; at intervals, the engineer had to pull a lever and literally blow off the steam to prevent an explosion.

In the 1830s, a locomotive was a thing of awe when quiet and still. A person who saw the iron monster blow off steam for the first time never forgot the incident.

Observers compared such an explosive incident with a sudden display of temper. Soon adopted into the speech of merchants and travelers, anyone indulging in a colorful outburst was said to "blow off steam."

FLY OFF THE HANDLE

If you've ever seen a person "fly off the handle," you may have been impressed at the energy and speed involved with that eruption of anger.

Early homesteaders found it hard to control their tempers when tools suddenly failed them. A common cause of such a turn of events was the shrinkage of wood—universally used for tool handles.

After having hung in a shed for months, the handle of a hoe or a rake was likely to come off after a few strokes. In the case of an ax, badly worn or shrunken wood is positively dangerous because the head of the tool can come loose at the first lick.

When the blade of an ax flies off the handle, it endangers the user and everyone standing nearby. That makes it almost as great a source of danger as a violent explosion of temper.

HOCUS POCUS

If you've ever played around with rhyming words, you are among company. This form of verbal recreation has been practiced for centuries in all cultures.

Early jugglers altered a Latin phrase used in the service of Holy Communion—a ritual in which ordinary bread is transformed. Magicians took the word *hocus* from classical terms for "Here is the body . . ."

Once that term had been coined for use in sleight-of-hand tricks, it was easy to form a rhyming partner. The result was *hocus pocus,* which means you had better pay close attention, or you will be badly fooled by what happens next.

LIVE WIRE

In the early days of household electricity, ordinary folks hardly knew anything about the newfangled way to control and use energy. Staring at a maze of wires, it was difficult or impossible for most people to fathom them.

Yet two things became common knowledge very early. Some wires carried no current and felt no different from anything else casually touched. But another wire in the same cluster would often yield a first-class jolt—or worse—when touched.

A wire of the latter kind was considered "live" because of the strong current in it. Some people are so full of energy that their blood seems to flow like an electrical current. Hence anyone who is always vibrant and ready to serve as the life of the party is known as a "live wire."

PULL THE PLUG

If financiers or authorities "pull the plug" on a project, there is a good chance it will go down the drain. Still, this way of expressing the idea of bringing something to an end is not indebted to round rubber plugs used in old-fashioned bathtubs.

Rather, it was the pulling of an electrical plug from an outlet that gave rise to the phrase. Borrowing from everyday experience, early in the electrical age it became common to express the idea of termination by using the phrase spawned by bringing early appliances and machines to a halt.

RAILROAD

Once the steam locomotive was found to be powerful and effective, the United States launched a binge of building. Hundreds of miles of track became thousands of miles in a short period.

Builders learned to push across rivers, through forests, and over mountains in an awesome fashion. It became understood that the railroad had to be built in a hurry, regardless of obstacles.

Pushing past difficulty in an erratic, disorderly manner spawned a phrase that has long outlasted the era in which it was first used. A person or group pushing an idea or an enterprise without regard for opposition is described as "railroading" it.

SIREN

French scientist Cagnard de la Tour experimented with sound for many years. In 1819 he invented a device designed to produce musical notes and measure their vibrations. Immersed in water, his gadget yielded a "singularly sweet and sonorous sound." At some speeds in the air it sounded almost like a human voice.

The name for this device was taken from Greek mythology.

The songs of the three sea nymphs, the Sirens, lured sailors to destruction. Since his sound maker sang under water, de la Tour borrowed from mythology and called it a *siren*.

Within fifty years the acoustical instrument found an unexpected use. Built to a larger scale, it served not to lure persons to destruction, but to warn them. Steam-powered sirens sitting on tall buildings signaled "Fire!" long before smaller ones mounted on ambulances and fire engines screamed "Get out of the way!"

WHISTLEBLOWER

A whistleblower who is interviewed for the television shows *60 Minutes* or *20/20* is likely to get results. Nuclear plants, suppliers of military hardware, and manufacturers of chemicals are prime targets for these people signaling wrongdoing.

The whistles of police are still heard in some cities. Their impact may have had a little influence in the formation of the modern title for an informer. However, action on the basketball court has been much more significant. Watch a game in the NCAA finals and count the number of times an official blows a whistle.

Most of the time, the sound of an official's whistle means "Stop instantly!"—which is the goal of the industrial or environmental whistleblower as well. The main object of whistleblowers is to stop illegal action and infringement on the rules of the game.

CHAPTER 19

SAY, DID YOU KNOW?

M uch of what we know about the origins of what we say and write can be found in the twenty volumes of the *Oxford English Dictionary*. A cursory glance at a few of its pages helps us to see how little we do know.

Nearly every word and phrase treated in this volume can be a conversation starter. Some that especially lend themselves to "Say, did you know . . . ?" are included in this section.

Band-Aid
Bury the Hatchet
Cracked Up

Go Bananas
Heart in the Right Place
Hype
Inside Track
Security Blanket
Sweetheart
True Blue
Wrong Side of the Bed

BAND-AID

In one report by the *Wall Street Journal,* experts were asked to cure a fiscal ill, and they spent a lot of time trying to make a diagnosis. Since they couldn't agree about the cause of the sickness, "all they did was to put a Band-Aid on it."

Even the head honcho of a big pharmaceutical company didn't anticipate that its ready-made bandage would make such a hit. Little bandages in a box solved minor household problems galore, but were useless in a major emergency. The popularity of Johnson & Johnson's Band-Aid caused its name to be associated with any small adhesive bandage and with patching up small injuries—as well as small problems.

BURY THE HATCHET

White trappers and soldiers in contact with American Indians on the frontier knew little about Native customs. In addition, most of them didn't care to learn.

White men mistakenly believed that the stone tomahawk

had no use except in battle. Among some tribes, ceremonial burial of a weapon signaled that a period of war had come to an end.

No tomahawk was remotely like a metal hatchet of the white man, and Indian weapons were given ceremonial interment only among a few cultures. Yet when an opponent ceases to fight or a spouse stops battling with words, he or she is still said to "bury the hatchet."

CRACKED UP

Sitting around the cracker barrel in a general store and swapping yarns, some idlers always evoked laughter. Others who told stories got only stares in response—the listeners didn't crack a smile.

Since hearty laughter constitutes a signal that a tale—or its teller—has hit the bull's-eye, cracked faces came to signify "first class." Once that usage was established, it was an easy step to label anything inferior as "not what it is cracked up to be."

GO BANANAS

What makes a person who is normally calm and quiet suddenly "go bananas"? Why do we specify this fruit instead of Granny Smith apples or Bose pears?

No one knows exactly why a person will act out in a given situation. But there's a good reason for saying that anyone temporarily out of control has "gone bananas." Actions of such a person are a lot like that of a caged monkey in a zoo. The sight of a keeper approaching with a bunch of bananas can make the animal freak out, or *go bananas*.

HEART IN THE RIGHT PLACE

Ancient Egyptian priests who prepared bodies for mummification knew a great deal about anatomy. During Europe's long Dark Ages, much of this lore was lost. Peasants who knew little about the body's internal organs were impressed by the rhythmic throbbing of big blood vessels—which often varied from person to person and even from time to time in the same person's arm or leg.

Variations in rate and intensity of throbbing were attributed to the heart wandering from its proper location. This literal belief produced a host of fanciful metaphors; an easily offended person was said "to wear his heart on his sleeve," and anyone mortally afraid was described as "having his heart in his mouth."

All of which means that a person whose heart is in the right place is properly constituted—and as a result is filled with good intentions.

HYPE

On the surface, there seems to be no logical reason why we should use *hype* to designate "high-pressure advertising." But ballyhoo from Madison Avenue or anywhere else is designed to affect behavior and decisions. That gives it a lot in common with mood-altering drugs.

During the 1920s, relatively mild narcotics were the most commonly available drugs for street use. Abbreviation of the hypodermic needle used to administer a drug created *hype* as a name for both an illegal drug and a state induced by it.

A carefully crafted promotional campaign is designed to alter attitudes and purchasing habits. Just as being "hyped up" by drugs might make one feel larger than life, so are a lot of ads just *hype*—exaggerated claims.

INSIDE TRACK

Anytime you're known to have the "inside track," a rival or competitor will acknowledge that you have the best of it. At least in its earliest usage, the expression had nothing to do with hidden or inside information.

As might be expected, the phrase comes from the racetrack.

Most contests of any length were held on oval or round tracks. Contestants waited for the signal to begin while spaced out along the starting line. Everyone knew that the person having the slot closest to the middle of the course had a good chance of running a shorter distance than rivals.

In a footrace the *inside track* was a major asset, and logically came to mean a strong advantage in any situation.

SECURITY BLANKET

Charles M. Schulz is famous as creator of the *Peanuts* comic strip and its characters. One of his claims to fame stems from coinage of the phrase *security blanket* to name any tangible object that soothes nerves and confers confidence.

As initially used by the writer-artist, the expression was literal. Linus, one of his characters, often appears holding a corner of a blanket that drags behind. While absence of that blanket means nervous apprehension, its presence symbolizes confidence and poise.

It is probable that, long before *Peanuts*, lots of mothers and fathers noticed that toddlers felt insecure without their favorite blankets. So the concept behind the phrase may be as old as the family. Still, the word pattern that identifies positive emotional effects of having a familiar object in hand may be strictly twentieth century in origin.

SWEETHEART

During the era when the longbow was the ultimate weapon, even physicians knew little about human anatomy. Pumping action of the heart caused it to be regarded as the seat of personality. Expressions paying tribute to this notion were probably literal rather than figurative. A person could be *hard-hearted*, *softhearted*, *lighthearted*, or *heavyhearted*.

In this climate of thought and speech, it was natural for a lover to refer to one who made the heart beat faster as a "swete hert" in Middle English. Separate terms were hyphenated for two or three centuries before *sweetheart* entered modern talk to label the sweet person who makes the heart throb.

TRUE BLUE

Cloth made by hand was long dyed in the household. Berries, bark, and a few blossoms yielded most of the coloring matter used to dye the cloth. Even when synthetic dyes came on the market, most of them were of inferior quality. Consequently, cloth often faded after a few washings.

Artisans of Coventry, England, discovered and kept secret a formula for the manufacture of a blue dye of superior quality. This Coventry blue—or "true blue"—remained bright after many washings.

For generations, *true blue* was absolutely the best that could be bought. From chatter of those who labored over dye vats and washtubs, the term entered general speech to stand for faithfulness and reliability of every sort.

WRONG SIDE OF THE BED

Nearly everything we use is shaped for right-handed people. Even a dexterous left-handed baseball pitcher may sometimes seem awkward. As a result, among the ancients the left side of the body (or the left side of anything else) was considered to be sinister—mysterious and dangerous, maybe even evil.

Old-time innkeepers often pushed the left sides of the bed against the walls so that guests could get up only on the right side.

Many who sleep in king- or queen-size modern beds attach little or no importance to the side that is used. But when a person shows unusual irritability or clumsiness, it may be called the result of having started the day by getting up on the "wrong side of the bed."

BIBLIOGRAPHY

More detailed information concerning most words and phrases in *Word Nerds Unite!* may be found in one or more of the following volumes. For the roots of standard English and American words, consult etymological dictionaries. By all odds the most valuable single work in print is the revised edition of the *Oxford English Dictionary*. Yet even this monumental work of scholarship omits numerous contemporary expressions that are American, rather than British.

Words and phrases not yet accepted as standard speech are treated in volumes dealing with slang. Many of these, but not all, appear in the *American Heritage Dictionary,* where brief hints concerning their origins are often included.

Adams, James T. *Dictionary of American History.* 7 vols. New York: Scribner's, 1940.

American Heritage Dictionary of the English Language. Rev. ed. New York: American Heritage, 1989.

Ammer, Christine. *Have a Nice Day—No Problem!: A Dictionary of Clichés*. New York: Dutton, 1992.

Ayto, John. *Dictionary of Word Origins*. New York: Arcade, 1990.

Barrere, A. *Argot and Slang*. London: Whittaker, 1887.

Bartlett, John R. *Dictionary of Americanisms*. Boston: Little, Brown, 1877.

Berliner, Barbara. *The Book of Answers*. New York: Prentice Hall, 1990.

Berrey, Lester V. and Melvin Van Den Bark, *The American Thesaurus of Slang*. New York: Crowell, 1962.

Bodmer, Frederick. *The Loom of Language*. New York: Norton, 1944.

Chambers, Robert. *The Book of Days*. Philadelphia: Lippincott, 1899.

Chapman, Robert L. *New Dictionary of American Slang*. New York: Harper, 1986.

Dickson, Paul. *Dickson's Word Treasury*. New York: John Wiley and Sons, 1992.

Evans, Bergan and Cornelia. *A Dictionary of Contemporary American Usage*. New York: Random House, 1957.

Farmer, John S. *Americanisms Old and New*. London: Poulter, 1889.

Farmer, John S. and W. E. Henley. *Slang and Its Analogues*. 7 vols. New Hyde Park: University Press, 1966.

Flexner, Stuart B. *I Hear America Talking*. New York: Van Nostrand, 1976.

———. *Listening to America*. New York: Simon and Schuster, 1982.

Funk, Charles E. *Heavens to Betsy!* New York: Warner Paperback Library, 1972.

_____. *Hereby Hangs A Tale.* New York: Warner Paperback Library, 1972.

_____. A *Hog on Ice.* New York: Warner Paperback Library, 1972.

_____. *Horsefeathers.* New York: Warner Paperback Library, 1972.

Goldin, Hyman E. *Dictionary of American Underworld Lingo.* New York: Twayne, 1950.

Granville, Wilfred. A *Dictionary of Sailors' Slang.* London: Deutsch, 1962.

Grun, Bernard. *The Timetables of History.* New York: Simon and Schuster, 1975.

Hargrove, Basil. *Origins and Meanings of Popular Phrases and Names.* Philadelphia: Lippincott, 1925.

Hendrickson, Robert. *The Dictionary of Eponyms.* New York: Dorset, 1972.

Hollander, Zander, ed. *The Encyclopedia of Sports Talk.* New York: Corwin, 1976.

Holt, Alfred H. *Phrase and Word Origins.* New York: Dover, 1961.

Hunt, Cecil. *Word Origins: The Romance of Language.* New York: Philosophical, 1949.

Lass, A. H.; Kiremidjian, D.; and Goldstein, R. M. *Dictionary of Classical, Biblical, and Literary Allusions.* New York: Facts on File Publications, 1987.

Manser, Martin. *Get to the Roots: A Dictionary of Word and Phrase Origins.* New York: Avon, 1990.

Matthews, Mitford M., ed. *Dictionary of Americanisms.* 2 vols. Chicago: University of Chicago Press, 1951.

Mencken, H. L. *The American Language*. 3 vols. New York: Knopf, 1936–48.

Morris, William and Mary. *Dictionary of Word and Phrase Origins*. 2 vols. New York: Harper, 1962–67.

Onions, C. T. *The Oxford Dictionary of English Etymology*. Oxford: Oxford University Press, 1966.

Oxford English Dictionary. 10 vols. Oxford: Oxford University Press, 1888–1935.

Oxford English Dictionary. Supp. 4 vols. R. W. Burchfield, ed. Oxford: Oxford University Press, 1987.

Oxford English Dictionary. 2d ed. 20 vols. J. A. Simpson and Edmund S. Weiner, eds. Oxford: Oxford University Press, 1989.

Partridge, Eric. *A Dictionary of Slang and Unconventional English*. New York: Macmillan, 1961.

_____. *A Dictionary of the Underworld*. New York: Macmillan, 1961.

_____. *Name Into Word*. London: Routledge, 1949.

_____. *Origins*. New York: Greenwich House, 1983.

Roback, Aaron A. *Dictionary of International Slurs*. Cambridge: Sci-Art, 1944.

Shipley, Joseph T. *Dictionary of Word Origins*. New York: Littlefield, 1967.

Skeat, Walter, W. *An Etymological Dictionary of the English Language*. Rev. ed. London: Oxford University Press, 1963.

Sorel, Nancy C. *Word People*. New York: American Heritage Press, 1970.

Webster's New World Dictionary of American English. 3d. coll. ed. New York: Webster's New World, 1988.

Weekley, Ernest. *Concise Etymological Dictionary of Modern English*. New York: Dutton, 1924.

_____. *The Romance of Names.* London: Murray, 1922.

_____. *The Romance of Words.* New York: Dover, 1961.

Wentworth, Harold and Stuart B. Flexner. *Dictionary of American Slang.* New York: Crowell, 1934.

Weseen, Maurice H., ed. *Dictionary of American Slang.* New York: Crowell, 1934.